AI-Powered Education

How Artificial Intelligence Is Transforming Teaching, Learning, and the Future of Schools

Written by
Eric LeBouthillier

AcraSolution | 2025 1st Edition
www.acrasolution.com

Preface

The classroom has always evolved — from chalkboards to smartboards, from textbooks to tablets. But we are now entering a far more transformative era, where artificial intelligence is not just an enhancement to learning, but a new layer of intelligence that changes *how* we teach, *how* students learn, and *how* schools operate.

I've written this book not as a futurist, but as someone who lives within the system — working in education and watching firsthand as our challenges grow: burnout, inequity, gaps in learning, disengagement. And yet, AI offers us not just a way out, but a way *forward.*

AI-Powered Education is your guide to understanding what's possible, what's working, and how to lead with confidence and ethics in this next chapter of learning. Whether you're a teacher, a tech leader, or a school administrator, this book will help you cut through the hype and focus on what actually matters: creating better outcomes for students.

— *Eric LeBouthillier*
Author & Cybersecurity Strategist

For permission requests or inquiries, contact the publisher through the website : www.acrasolution.com

LEGAL DISCLAIMER

This eBook is provided for informational purposes only and does not constitute legal, financial, or professional advice. The author and publisher have made every reasonable effort to ensure the accuracy and completeness of the information contained herein; however, neither assumes any responsibility for errors, omissions, or contrary interpretations of the subject matter.

Readers are encouraged to consult with qualified professionals for specific advice tailored to their individual needs. The mention of any products, services, or third-party entities does not imply an endorsement or guarantee of their effectiveness or suitability. Any application of the strategies and recommendations presented is at the reader's discretion and risk.

The author and publisher shall not be liable for any damages (including, without limitation, direct, indirect, incidental, or consequential) caused by the use, misuse, or interpretation of the information herein. All references to regulatory standards, statutes, or compliance requirements are informational and do not replace official legal counsel.

By reading and applying the concepts in this eBook, you acknowledge that you bear sole responsibility for the outcomes of your decisions and actions. If you do not agree to these terms, please discontinue use of this publication immediately.

Who This Book Is For

This book is for:

- **K-12 and post-secondary educators** exploring how AI can personalize instruction and improve engagement
- **School administrators and principals** looking to modernize systems, reduce workloads, and lead innovation
- **IT and EdTech leaders** tasked with evaluating AI tools and making data-safe decisions
- **Education policymakers** interested in building fair, ethical frameworks around AI in public institutions
- **Parents and advocates** who want to understand how AI will shape their child's educational experience

Whether you're skeptical or excited, this book gives you a grounded, real-world lens on what AI can do — and what it should never be allowed to do — in schools.

Table of Contents

CHAPTER 1: THE CRISIS IN EDUCATION — AND WHY AI IS THE ANSWER 15

Rising Demands, Shrinking Resources, and Post-Pandemic Exhaustion 16

The Limits of Traditional Edtech 16

Why AI Isn't Hype — It's a Systems-Level Shift 17

Real-World Example: Finland's National AI Curriculum Rollout 18

Tactical Best Practices 19

Common Pitfalls or Mistakes 19

Checklist-Style Action Steps 20

CHAPTER 2: WHAT AI IN EDUCATION REALLY MEANS 22

Clear Breakdown of AI, ML, NLP, and Computer Vision 23

AI vs Automation vs Personalization 24

Myths Debunked: "AI Will Replace Teachers" 25

Visual: AI Use Cases Mapped to Classroom Functions 25

Tactical Best Practices 27

Common Pitfalls to Avoid 27

Checklist-Style Action Steps 27

CHAPTER 3: PERSONALIZED LEARNING AT SCALE..... 29

How AI Understands the Learner 30
Adaptive Learning Algorithms 30
Micro-Profiling of Learners 30
Real-Time Feedback and Course Correction 30

Tools Leading the Charge 31
Khan Academy + GPT 31
Century Tech (UK) 32

Real-World Example: National Adoption in Schools 32
What Happened 32
What Went Right or Wrong 33
What We Learn from It 33

Tactical Best Practices for Schools and EdTech Teams 34

Common Pitfalls to Avoid 34

Checklist: Implementing Personalized AI Learning 35

CHAPTER 4: AI-POWERED ASSESSMENT AND GRADING 36

What AI Can (and Can't) Do in Assessment 37
Auto-Grading at Scale 37
Plagiarism Detection and Originality Checking 37
Formative Feedback, Instantly 38

Where Bias Creeps In (and How to Guard Against It) 39
Common Sources of AI Grading Bias 39
How to Mitigate 39

Workflow: Blended AI + Human Feedback Cycle 40

Real-World Example: District-Wide AI Grading Pilot 41
What Happened 41
What Went Right or Wrong 41
What We Learn from It 41

Tactical Best Practices for Educators and EdTech Leaders 42

Common Pitfalls to Avoid **42**

Checklist: Building a Responsible AI Grading System **42**

CHAPTER 5: AI IN SPECIAL EDUCATION AND ACCESSIBILITY 44

From Accommodation to Empowerment **45**
- Speech-to-Text and Text-to-Speech 45
- Emotion-Aware Tutoring Bots 45

Empowering Neurodiverse and Non-Verbal Learners **46**
- Tailored Interfaces and Pacing 46
- Visual and Non-Verbal Expression Tools 47

Real-World Example: Microsoft's Accessibility AI Tools **47**
- What Happened 47
- What Went Right or Wrong 48
- What We Learn from It 48

Tactical Best Practices for Schools and Developers **49**

Common Pitfalls to Avoid **49**

Checklist: Building Inclusive Classrooms with AI **49**

CHAPTER 6: REDEFINING THE TEACHER'S ROLE IN AN AI WORLD 51

From Knowledge Dispenser to Learning Architect **52**
- New Core Roles for the AI-Era Teacher 52
- Teaching in an AI-Rich Environment 52

Training Teachers to Work With AI, Not Fear It **53**
- The Professional Development Gap 53
- Principles for Empowering Teacher Training 53

Real-World Example: Teacher Transformation in Singapore **54**
- What Happened 54
- What Went Right or Wrong 55

What We Learn from It 55

Tactical Best Practices for School Leaders and Teacher Trainers 56

Common Pitfalls to Avoid 56

Checklist: Supporting the Teacher Role in an AI World 57

CHAPTER 7: SMART CLASSROOMS AND THE RISE OF LEARNING ANALYTICS 58

What Makes a Classroom “Smart”? 59
Core Technologies in Smart Classrooms 59

Real-Time Feedback and Predictive Power 60
Real-Time Feedback Loops 60
Predictive Analytics in Action 60

Tools Leading the Movement 61
Classcraft 61
BrightBytes 61
Edsby 62

Real-World Example: District-Wide Engagement Monitoring 62
What Happened 62
What Went Right or Wrong 63
What We Learn from It 63

Tactical Best Practices for Leaders and Developers 63

Common Pitfalls to Avoid 64

Checklist: Building a Smart, Data-Driven Classroom 64

CHAPTER 8: THE ETHICAL AI CLASSROOM 66

Why Ethics Can’t Be an Afterthought 67

Four Core Pillars of Ethical AI Use in Schools 68
1. Consent and Transparency 68

2. Data Privacy 68
3. Fairness and Bias Prevention 68
4. Explainability and Accountability 69

Building Digital Citizenship into the Curriculum 69
Core Concepts for K–12 AI Literacy 70

The AI Bill of Rights for Schools 70
AI Bill of Rights (for Schools and Students) 70

Tactical Best Practices for School Leaders and EdTech Teams 71

Common Pitfalls to Avoid 72

Checklist: Ethics Readiness in the AI Classroom 72

CHAPTER 9: CHATGPT IN SCHOOLS — USE IT OR BLOCK IT? 74

The Debate: Blocker vs. Innovator 75
Common Fears 75
Missed Opportunities 75

Safe, Structured Ways to Use ChatGPT in the Classroom 76
Pedagogically Aligned Use Cases 76

Classroom Prompt Library (By Grade Level and Subject) 77
Elementary (Grades 3–5) 77
Middle School (Grades 6–8) 77
High School (Grades 9–12) 77

Principal's Guide to Writing a ChatGPT Policy 78
Key Policy Elements 79

Tactical Best Practices for Teachers and Leaders 80

Common Pitfalls to Avoid 80

Checklist: Launching a School-Wide ChatGPT Strategy 81

CHAPTER 10: AI AND STUDENT MENTAL HEALTH MONITORING 82

Where AI Can Help: Early Detection and Scalable Support 83
Key Capabilities 83

Where It Overreaches: Risks and Boundaries 84
Top Concerns 84

Real-World Example: Stanford's AI Well-Being Pilot 85
What Happened 85
What Went Right or Wrong 85
What We Learn from It 85

Red Lines: Non-Negotiables in Mental Health AI 86
Red Line 1: No Surveillance Without Consent 86
Red Line 2: AI Never Replaces Human Judgment 86
Red Line 3: Transparent Access to Records 86
Red Line 4: Cultural Sensitivity Must Be Built In 86
Red Line 5: Wellness ≠ Discipline 86

Tactical Best Practices for Schools Considering Mental Health AI 88

Common Pitfalls to Avoid 88

Checklist: Responsible AI Mental Health Use 88

CHAPTER 11: AI FOR SCHOOL OPERATIONS AND ADMINISTRATION 90

Where Schools Waste Time and Resources 91

Core Use Cases for AI in School Operations 91
1. Automated Scheduling 91
2. Budget Forecasting and Optimization 92
3. Human Resources Automation 92
4. Smart Procurement and Inventory 92

Tools Leading the Charge 93
IBM Watson for Education (Ops Module) 93

PowerSchool Predictive Suite 94

Principal Testimonials: Efficiency That Frees Up Time....94

Tactical Best Practices for AI-Driven School Operations....95

Common Pitfalls to Avoid....96

Checklist: Building AI-Ready School Operations 96

CHAPTER 12: BUILDING AN AI-READY SCHOOL CULTURE 98

Why Culture Eats Strategy (and Tech) for Breakfast....99
Core Cultural Barriers to AI Adoption 99

Training and Buy-In: Where True Adoption Begins 100
What Works....100
What Doesn't 100

School-Wide PD Blueprint for AI Integration 101
Phase 1: Awareness and Framing (Month 1–3)....101
Phase 2: Skills and Use Cases (Month 4–6)....101
Phase 3: Coaching and Scaling (Month 7–12) 101

The 12-Month AI-Readiness Roadmap 101
Q1: Explore....101
Q2: Experiment....102
Q3: Evaluate 102
Q4: Expand....102

Tactical Best Practices for Building AI-Ready Culture 103

Common Pitfalls to Avoid....103

Checklist: Is Your School Culture AI-Ready?....103

CHAPTER 13: EQUITY AND AI IN PUBLIC EDUCATION 105

The Digital Divide in the Age of AI 106

Risks for Rural and Low-Income Schools 107
Common Barriers 107
Hidden Cost of Inequity 107

What Works: Funding Models and Strategic Partnerships 107
1. Public–Private Partnerships 108
2. State-Level AI Innovation Grants 108
3. Local Foundations and Nonprofits 108

Real-World Example: Rural AI Integration in Kentucky 109
What Happened 109
What Went Right 109
What We Learn from It 110

Policy Gaps That Need Fixing 110
Current Gaps 110
What Advocates Can Do 110

Tactical Best Practices for Equity-Driven AI Integration 111

Common Pitfalls to Avoid 112

Checklist: Making AI Work for Every Learner 112

CHAPTER 14: LEADING THE SHIFT — TRAITS OF AI-FORWARD EDUCATORS 113

Who Are AI-Forward Educators? 114
Core Traits 114

Creating AI Champions in Your School 115
How to Identify a Champion 115
How to Support Them 115

Microtraining That Scales 115
Microtraining Best Practices 116

Case Study: The "AI Lunch & Learn" Movement 117

What Happened 117
What Went Right 117
What We Learn from It 117

Tactical Best Practices for Cultivating AI-Forward Leadership 118

Common Pitfalls to Avoid 119

Checklist: Building a Network of AI-Forward Educators 119

CHAPTER 15: THE FUTURE OF EDUCATION — AND HOW TO LEAD IT 121

The Tech Stack of Tomorrow's Classrooms 122
AI + AR/VR + IoT + Blockchain 122

Predictive Pathways: Career Mapping and Microcredentials 123
Predictive Career Mapping 123
Microcredentials and Global Access 123

The 5-Year Strategic Plan for School Leaders 124
Year 1: Vision + Audit 124
Year 2: Pilot + Feedback 124
Year 3: Scale + Align 125
Year 4: Integrate + Report 125
Year 5: Sustain + Lead 125

Final Message: The Transformation Is Already Here 127

Bonus – FREE eBook Version 135

Chapter 1: The Crisis in Education — and Why AI Is the Answer

The education sector is straining under a load it was never designed to carry. As student needs grow more complex and teacher burnout accelerates, schools and institutions are left trying to do more with less — and in many cases, falling behind. Traditional solutions aren't failing because of lack of effort; they're failing because they weren't built for this era. Meanwhile, artificial intelligence (AI) is stepping into the spotlight — not as a novelty, but as a structural shift.

This chapter outlines why AI isn't just "another edtech fad," but a system-level response to the compounding pressures in education. We'll unpack what's broken, why past fixes haven't worked, and how AI — when deployed thoughtfully — can help schools, teachers, and students reclaim their capacity to succeed.

Rising Demands, Shrinking Resources, and Post-Pandemic Exhaustion

If you work in or with education, you already know the squeeze. Expectations have never been higher — yet the resources to meet them are flatlining or in decline.

- **Teacher shortages** are now a national issue, not a localized challenge. Many districts report 20% vacancy rates for core subject areas.
- **Mental health crises** among students are rising, leaving teachers to double as counselors, often without proper training or support.
- **Remote learning gaps** from the pandemic remain unclosed. Some students lost more than a year of academic progress — and it's teachers who are expected to recover that ground.
- **Administrative burden** has exploded. From lesson tracking to parent communication to compliance paperwork, educators now spend nearly half their time on non-teaching tasks.

This isn't just a capacity problem — it's an exhaustion crisis. And band-aid solutions like digital worksheets and video calls are no longer enough.

The Limits of Traditional Edtech

Edtech promised to modernize learning. And in many ways, it has. Tools like online grading platforms, virtual classrooms, and interactive lesson builders have become table stakes. But there's a ceiling to what traditional edtech can deliver:

- It digitizes tasks but doesn't reduce them.
- It centralizes information but doesn't interpret it.
- It enhances access but not necessarily equity.

In short, most edtech improves the interface, not the outcome. It assumes the human system beneath it can scale endlessly — and that's simply not true.

Worse, some systems increase complexity without adding value. Teachers are expected to navigate a patchwork of disconnected platforms, leading to duplication, confusion, and frustration. What's needed now isn't more tools — it's smarter infrastructure.

Why AI Isn't Hype — It's a Systems-Level Shift

AI in education doesn't mean humanoid robots or automated classrooms. It means applying intelligent systems to do what people shouldn't have to — so educators can do what only they can.

Here's what makes AI different from conventional edtech:

- **Personalization at scale**: Adaptive learning platforms use AI to adjust content difficulty, pacing, and feedback for each learner — something a human can't do for 30 students at once.
- **Administrative offloading**: AI can automate routine tasks like attendance tracking, email sorting, and progress alerts, giving educators back hours per week.
- **Insight generation**: Natural language processing (NLP) tools can scan student writing to identify comprehension gaps, emotional tone, or engagement trends across an entire cohort.

This isn't just automation — it's amplification. When thoughtfully implemented, AI becomes the infrastructure that supports sustainable education at scale. Not by replacing humans, but by enabling them to focus where they matter most: connection, insight, and mentorship.

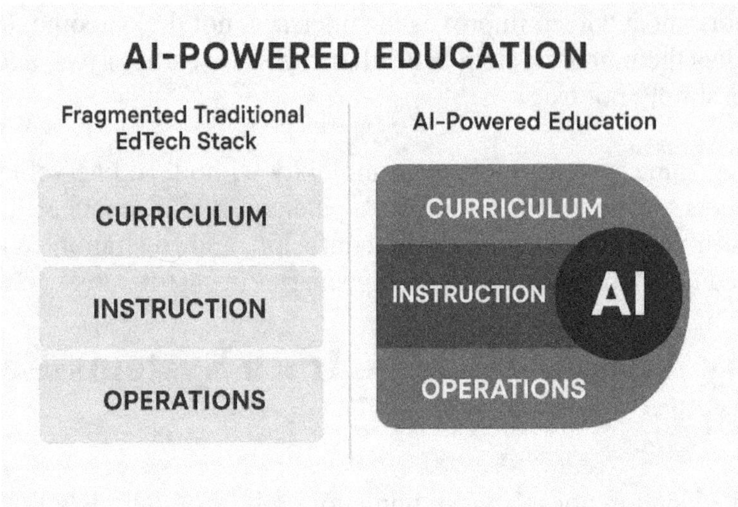

Real-World Example: Finland's National AI Curriculum Rollout

What Happened
Finland, widely regarded for its forward-thinking education system, launched an ambitious initiative in 2018: to teach AI literacy to every citizen — starting with schools. Their goal was not to train programmers, but to empower all students with a functional understanding of AI's role in society.

What Went Right

- **Public-private collaboration**: The curriculum was developed with input from universities, industry leaders, and educators — ensuring it was both rigorous and relatable.
- **Modular content**: Courses like *Elements of AI* were designed for self-paced learning and adapted for middle and high school classrooms.
- **Accessibility first**: All materials were made freely available, with multilingual support, including for adult learners and teachers themselves.

What We Learn From It

- AI isn't just for STEM. Finland embedded AI education into civics, language arts, and ethics — recognizing that its impact is cultural, not just technical.
- Empowering educators is critical. The initiative invested heavily in teacher training and support networks.
- Curriculum reform can be inclusive. By starting early and making learning universal, Finland avoided the digital divide that so often accompanies new tech adoption.

This case illustrates what's possible when AI is treated not as a bolt-on tool, but as a foundational literacy for the next generation.

Tactical Best Practices

- **Start with staff, not students**: Teachers need time, training, and tools to trust AI's role in the classroom.
- **Use AI to simplify, not complicate**: Focus on workflows where AI reduces noise — like auto-grading or scheduling — not ones that add layers of oversight.
- **Choose platforms that adapt**: Avoid "one-size-fits-all" software. Look for tools that adjust to learners' behavior and performance.
- **Pilot in small groups**: Test AI-driven learning with one class or grade level before scaling.

Common Pitfalls or Mistakes

- **Treating AI as a silver bullet**: No tool solves systemic inequity or policy-level underfunding.
- **Neglecting ethical considerations**: Data privacy, algorithmic bias, and student profiling must be addressed early — not after rollout.

- **Skipping training**: Expecting staff to adopt AI without clear guidance leads to abandonment or misuse.
- **Chasing trends**: What's flashy isn't always effective. Focus on value, not novelty.

Checklist-Style Action Steps

- Audit where staff time is going: What non-teaching tasks dominate the week?
- Identify 1–2 AI-enabled tools that target those exact pain points.
- Set clear success metrics: Time saved, engagement boosted, outcomes improved.
- Schedule PD sessions focused on *application*, not theory.
- Create opt-in pilot programs with built-in feedback loops.
- Document results and refine before full deployment.

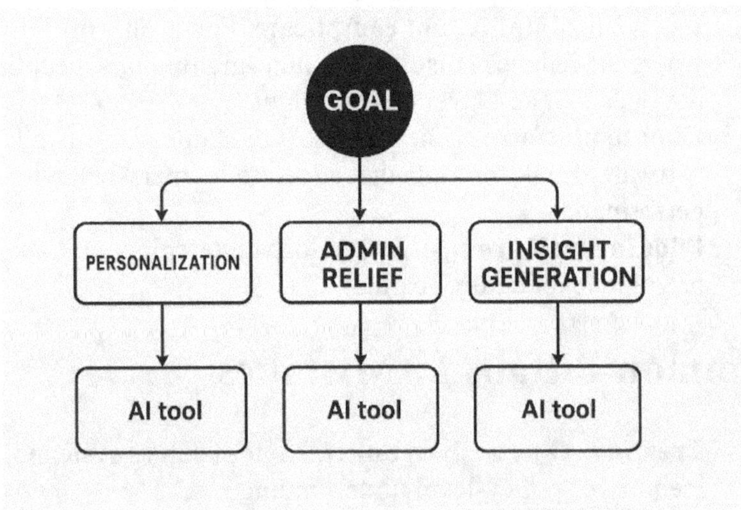

Conclusion

Education isn't just at a crossroads — it's at a breaking point. The post-pandemic landscape has made it clear: we cannot teach, manage, or scale learning in the same way we did a decade ago. What's needed now isn't more apps or dashboards — it's intelligent systems that relieve the burden, restore teacher agency, and help students thrive in complexity.

Artificial intelligence, when implemented with care and clarity, isn't just a fix — it's an upgrade to the system itself. One that finally aligns with the real demands educators face every day.

Next Steps

Now that we've unpacked why AI isn't optional in modern education, it's time to get specific. In **Chapter 2: What AI in Education Really Means**, we'll strip away the jargon and lay out — in plain terms — what AI, machine learning, and natural language processing actually *do* in the classroom. You'll walk away ready to spot the hype, understand the tech, and lead with confidence.

Chapter 2: What AI in Education Really Means

Artificial intelligence is reshaping how learning happens — but for many educators and school leaders, the term still feels abstract. What exactly is AI doing in classrooms? Is it just automation with a fancier name? Or something fundamentally different?

This chapter breaks it all down. You'll walk away with a clear understanding of AI's core technologies — what they are, what they're not, and how they map to everyday classroom needs. We'll also tackle a persistent fear head-on: No, AI is not here to replace teachers. It's here to extend their impact.

Clear Breakdown of AI, ML, NLP, and Computer Vision

Before we explore what AI *does*, we need to define what it *is* — in plain English. Here's a simplified snapshot of the core components driving most educational AI systems:

- **Artificial Intelligence (AI)**: Any system that mimics human intelligence — making decisions, solving problems, or learning from data.
- **Machine Learning (ML)**: A subset of AI where algorithms "learn" from patterns in data. Instead of being explicitly programmed, ML models adjust their behavior over time.
- **Natural Language Processing (NLP)**: This allows software to understand and generate human language — spoken or written. Think essay feedback, voice-to-text, or even chatbots that answer student questions.
- **Computer Vision**: This gives machines the ability to interpret visual information, like handwritten homework, gestures, or facial expressions during a virtual lesson.

AI ARTIFICIAL INTELLIGENCE	ML MACHINE LEARNING	NLP NATURAL LANGUAGE PROCESSING	COMPUTER VISION
Scheduling classes	Identifying grading patterns	Generating feedback	Virtual proctoring

Each of these tools serves a unique function — but when combined, they create intelligent systems that can adapt to students, reduce teacher load, and personalize the entire learning experience.

AI vs Automation vs Personalization

It's easy to confuse these terms — especially when vendors use them interchangeably. But in practice, they mean very different things:

- **Automation** is task-based. It follows rules to reduce repetitive work (e.g., sending reminders or scoring quizzes).
- **AI** is decision-based. It adjusts to context — like flagging a student at risk based on performance trends.
- **Personalization** is outcome-based. It adapts the experience — what a student sees next depends on what they just did.

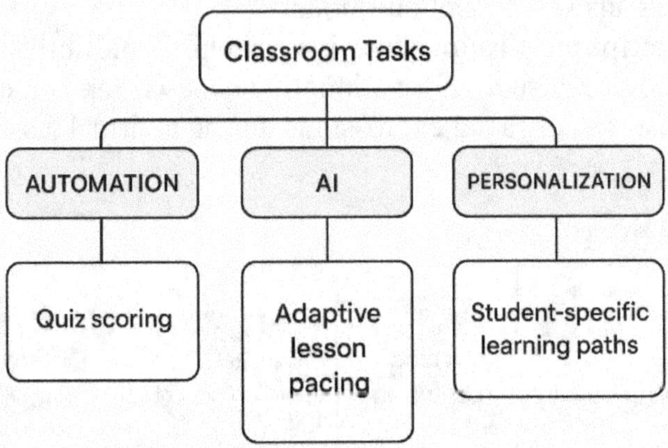

Think of automation as helpful, but static. AI is responsive — and personalization is the ultimate goal: giving each student exactly what they need, when they need it.

Myths Debunked: "AI Will Replace Teachers"

Let's address the elephant in the room. One of the most common — and misguided — fears about AI in education is that it will somehow make teachers obsolete.

Here's why that's not just false, but fundamentally backwards:

- **AI handles scale, not care.** It can grade 100 essays or monitor pacing for 300 students — but it can't inspire curiosity, manage conflict, or build trust.
- **AI provides signals, not wisdom.** It can surface which students are stuck — but not *why* they're struggling or how to support them emotionally.
- **AI amplifies, not replaces.** The best AI tools are co-pilots, not captains. They surface data, free time, and personalize learning — so educators can focus on what only humans can do.

The future isn't teacher-less. It's teacher-empowered.

Visual: AI Use Cases Mapped to Classroom Functions

To make this even clearer, here's a visual summary of where and how AI can support different layers of the educational experience.

Classroom Function	AI Technology Used	Example Use Case
Lesson Planning	ML + NLP	Suggests resources based on standards and goals
Student Assessment	NLP + CV	Analyzes open-ended answers, flags plagiarism

Classroom Function	AI Technology Used	Example Use Case
Engagement Monitoring	Computer Vision + ML	Tracks attentiveness in remote learning settings
Content Delivery	Personalization Engine	Recommends next modules based on mastery
Communication	NLP	Summarizes class activity for parent reports
Administrative Tasks	Automation	Handles attendance, grade sync, reminder emails

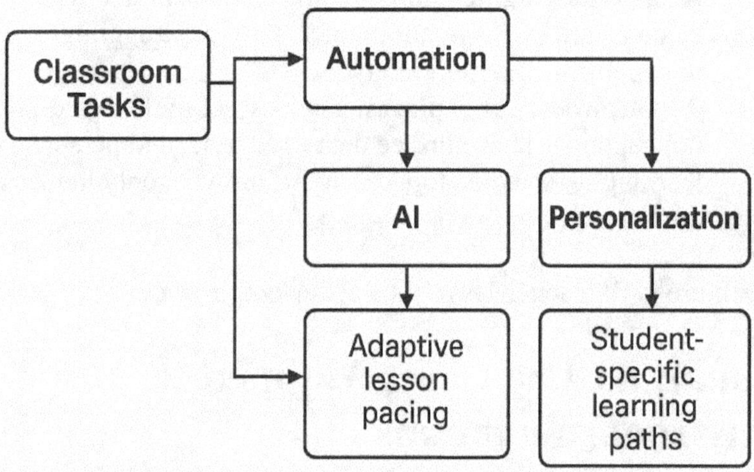

This crosswalk isn't theoretical — it's already happening. Many schools are piloting or scaling tools with these functions baked in.

Tactical Best Practices

- **Clarify goals before selecting tools**: What challenge are you trying to solve — grading burden? Engagement tracking? Personalized pacing?
- **Start with low-stakes use cases**: Document processing, quiz analysis, or parent alerts are great entry points.
- **Train staff on what AI is — and isn't**: Demystify the tools. Fear shrinks when understanding grows.
- **Keep humans in the loop**: AI should inform decisions, not make them unilaterally.

Common Pitfalls to Avoid

- **Treating AI as a buzzword**: Tools that don't adapt, learn, or predict aren't really AI — they're just software.
- **Skipping integration**: AI tools that don't sync with your LMS or grading system create more work, not less.
- **Ignoring equity**: If training data is biased, outcomes will be too. Choose vendors with a commitment to fairness and transparency.
- **Under-communicating with families**: Let parents know how AI supports — not monitors — their child.

Checklist-Style Action Steps

- Inventory which staff tasks are most time-consuming or repetitive.
- Identify AI tools that target those pain points with clear ROI.
- Run a short pilot (4–6 weeks) with teacher opt-in and feedback loops.
- Provide basic AI literacy PD for your team — no jargon, just clarity.
- Track early wins and blockers to refine deployment strategy.

Conclusion

Understanding what AI *really* is — and what it isn't — is the first step toward using it well. When we strip away the buzzwords and look at practical functions, the value becomes obvious: AI is here to make education more human, not less.

By automating the menial and surfacing the meaningful, AI gives teachers back their most precious resources: time, energy, and insight.

Next Steps

Now that you know what AI does under the hood, we'll explore its most powerful application to date: personalization. In **Chapter 3: Personalized Learning at Scale**, we'll show how tools like Khan Academy, GPT, and Squirrel AI are customizing education in real time — and what it takes to make that scalable, equitable, and effective.

Chapter 3: Personalized Learning at Scale

The modern classroom is evolving fast, but not fast enough for every student. For decades, education systems have struggled with a one-size-fits-all approach. Teachers do their best with the resources they have, but the truth remains: students learn at different paces, with different needs, and in different ways. When instruction fails to adapt to these differences, performance gaps widen, and engagement drops.

This is where artificial intelligence steps in—not as a replacement for educators, but as a force multiplier. AI-driven personalized learning is changing how we address individual strengths, weaknesses, and learning styles, not just in theory, but in real-world classrooms at scale.

When implemented well, AI helps ensure that no student falls through the cracks, even in overcrowded schools or under-resourced districts. In this chapter, we'll explore how personalization works under the hood, the tools making it real, and what we can learn from large-scale rollouts around the world.

How AI Understands the Learner

At the heart of AI-based personalization is a dynamic feedback loop: the system continuously collects data on student performance, behavior, and preferences, then uses that data to adapt instruction in real time. But how exactly does it tailor learning?

Adaptive Learning Algorithms

These algorithms adjust content difficulty based on student responses. If a learner breezes through a topic, the system introduces more challenging material. If they struggle, it circles back with simpler explanations or alternate formats—videos, simulations, quizzes—based on what worked previously.

Micro-Profiling of Learners

AI doesn't just look at scores. It builds detailed learner profiles, factoring in:

- Time spent per question
- Error patterns
- Preferred learning modalities (text vs. video vs. interactive tasks)
- Attention span indicators

These profiles drive content sequencing and pacing for each student.

Real-Time Feedback and Course Correction

Unlike traditional instruction, where feedback loops are slow and reactive, AI enables real-time correction. A student who misunderstands a key math concept isn't left behind until test day—they get targeted reinforcement immediately.

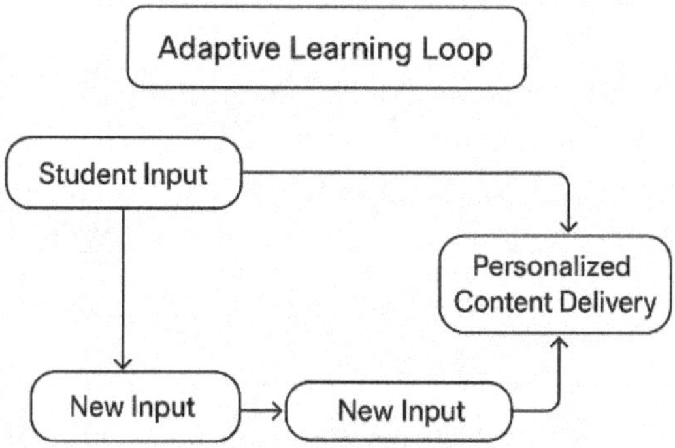

Tools Leading the Charge

AI-powered learning isn't a futuristic dream—it's already reshaping classrooms via platforms that are user-friendly, scalable, and backed by research. Here are three leading examples:

Khan Academy + GPT

Khan Academy's integration of GPT-4 under the "Khanmigo" pilot offers conversational tutoring that adjusts to student responses. Whether a learner is tackling algebra or history, the AI coach guides them step-by-step, explains concepts in simpler terms, and even encourages metacognitive reflection ("What did you notice about how you solved that?").

Squirrel AI (China)

Squirrel AI is one of the most advanced adaptive learning systems globally, used by millions of students across China. Its strength lies in ultra-granular diagnostics: breaking down knowledge into atomic units and identifying specific gaps (e.g., not just "bad at fractions," but misunderstanding of reciprocal operations within mixed-number division).

Century Tech (UK)

Century blends neuroscience with machine learning. It personalizes content while giving teachers analytics dashboards that highlight which students need help, with what, and when. It's particularly valued for integrating teacher-driven oversight with AI automation.

	Khanmigo	Squirrel AI	CENTURY Tech
Learner Adaptation	Personalized tutoring	Adaptive lesson paths	Individualized learning journeys
Data Used	Past questions & answers	Responses & behavior data	Learner performance & cognitive ability
Teacher Integration	Tool for teacher support	Monitoring & intervention	Planning & intervention

Real-World Example: National Adoption in Schools

What Happened

In 2019, a major school district in the U.S. piloted an AI-powered adaptive learning program across 25 middle schools. Simultaneously, China's Ministry of Education partnered with Squirrel AI to implement personalized tutoring in thousands of classrooms. Both projects sought to close learning gaps using AI.

What Went Right or Wrong

In China, results were dramatic. Test scores in pilot schools improved up to 30% over control groups, and teachers reported better engagement and retention. In the U.S., results were mixed: some schools saw gains, others struggled with teacher adoption. A common friction point? Teachers felt sidelined or undertrained in interpreting AI data.

What We Learn from It

AI is only as effective as the ecosystem around it. China's rollout included intensive teacher training and curriculum alignment. In contrast, the U.S. effort often lacked proper change management. The lesson: personalized learning works best when educators are empowered, not replaced.

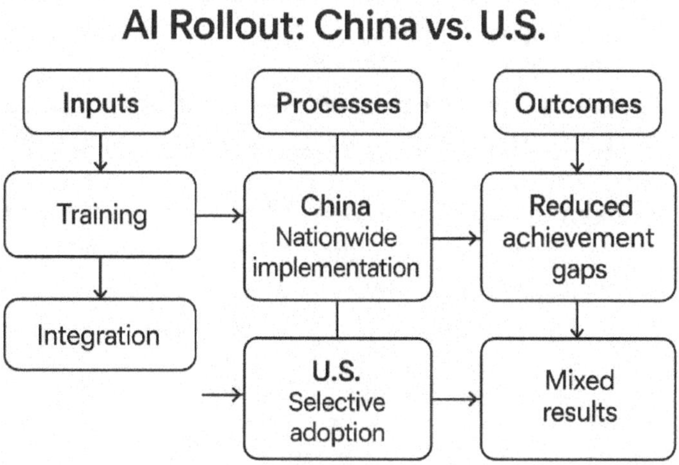

Tactical Best Practices for Schools and EdTech Teams

- **Start with clear pedagogy.** Choose tools that align with your teaching goals, not just flashy features.
- **Train teachers deeply.** AI insights are only useful if educators know how to act on them.
- **Use AI for diagnostics, not decision-making.** Let AI surface gaps; let humans decide interventions.
- **Respect privacy boundaries.** Ensure data collection complies with FERPA, GDPR, or relevant local laws.
- **Blend human and machine feedback.** Use AI for scale, teachers for nuance.

Common Pitfalls to Avoid

- **Over-reliance on the AI's accuracy.** No algorithm perfectly models a human learner. Cross-check with teacher observation.
- **Assuming personalization = isolation.** AI-driven pathways must still allow for group work, discussion, and peer interaction.
- **Neglecting equity in access.** AI-powered platforms require devices, bandwidth, and digital literacy—not all students have equal footing.

Checklist: Implementing Personalized AI Learning

- Identify learning gaps you want to address
- Choose a platform that supports your curriculum
- Assess device and connectivity readiness
- Create a rollout plan with teacher PD (professional development)
- Define metrics for success (e.g., engagement, mastery)
- Establish a feedback loop between teachers and tech teams
- Review and update student privacy and data policies

Conclusion

AI-driven personalization is not a silver bullet, but it's a powerful lever—if implemented with care. When adaptive learning tools are used to amplify what teachers already do well, the classroom becomes more inclusive, responsive, and effective. For SMBs in EdTech or school districts looking to innovate, the lesson is clear: AI should serve the learner *and* the educator, equally.

Next Steps

If you're exploring AI in education, the next critical frontier is assessment. Personalized instruction is only half the equation; measuring progress is the other. In **Chapter 4: AI-Powered Assessment and Grading**, we'll break down how automation is reshaping feedback, evaluation, and accountability—without losing the human touch.

Chapter 4: AI-Powered Assessment and Grading

Grades carry weight. For students, they shape self-esteem, scholarships, and futures. For educators, they reflect performance, pace, and progress. And for administrators, they're the data behind decisions. But in today's fast-moving classrooms, the act of grading is overwhelmed—by volume, variability, and the growing demand for meaningful feedback. Traditional systems are stretched thin, and that's where AI-powered assessment steps in.

Done right, AI doesn't just reduce grading time—it improves fairness, consistency, and immediacy. It also helps teachers reclaim their role as facilitators, not data clerks. But these benefits come with real risks. Automated decisions can be biased, impersonal, or poorly understood. In this chapter, we'll break down where AI makes sense in assessment, where human judgment must stay central, and how to build workflows that blend the best of both.

What AI Can (and Can't) Do in Assessment

AI assessment tools fall into three core functions: **auto-grading**, **plagiarism detection**, and **formative feedback generation**. Each offers major advantages—but none are plug-and-play solutions.

Auto-Grading at Scale

AI can rapidly grade multiple-choice, short-answer, and increasingly, even long-form writing. Natural Language Processing (NLP) models are now trained to evaluate grammar, structure, coherence, and argument strength. They recognize keyword patterns and scoring rubrics. But nuance still trips them up.

What works:

- Standardized quizzes and math problem sets
- Short written responses with clear rubrics
- Peer-assessment assisted by AI scoring

What doesn't:

- Creative writing, poetry, or personal narrative
- Culturally nuanced or metaphor-rich content
- Context-sensitive argumentation

Plagiarism Detection and Originality Checking

Modern tools go far beyond checking copy-paste violations. They evaluate paraphrasing, idea overlap, and even AI-generated content. Leading platforms like Turnitin now include AI writing detection flags to alert teachers when something feels… off.

Caveat: These systems aren't foolproof. False positives can mislabel honest work, and false negatives miss subtle violations. That's why AI should assist, not decide.

Formative Feedback, Instantly

Some AI tools generate instant, personalized feedback for students. They highlight errors, suggest improvements, or prompt reflection. For teachers, this is a game-changer—freeing up time for richer classroom interaction.

Done well, AI feedback is:

- Timely: provided within moments of submission
- Specific: targeting clear improvements
- Scalable: delivered to large cohorts without burnout

Done poorly, it's generic, unclear, or even discouraging. This is where human review becomes critical.

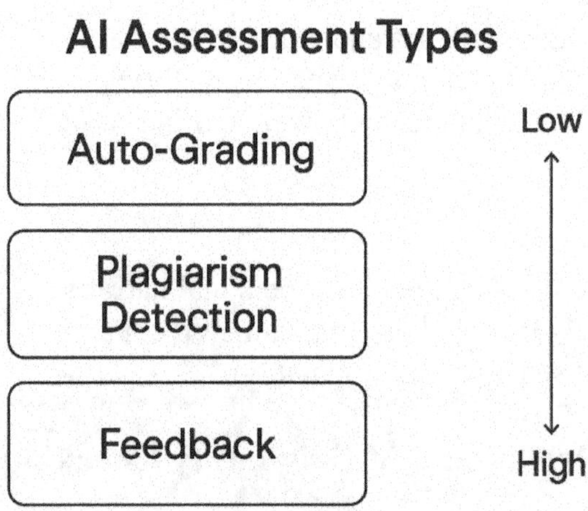

Where Bias Creeps In (and How to Guard Against It)

Automated grading isn't neutral. Every model is trained on data—and that data reflects human assumptions, preferences, and blind spots. This can result in systemic disadvantages for students from diverse backgrounds, especially in writing-intensive assessments.

Common Sources of AI Grading Bias

- **Linguistic bias:** Penalizing non-native English patterns or dialects
- **Cultural bias:** Misinterpreting references outside the training data
- **Format bias:** Preferring certain essay structures over others
- **Access bias:** Rewarding students trained in test-taking over knowledge

How to Mitigate

- Always use AI grading as a *first pass*, not a final word
- Review flagged work manually, especially when performance deviates from the norm
- Customize rubrics to reflect local pedagogy and diversity
- Involve diverse educators in model training and validation

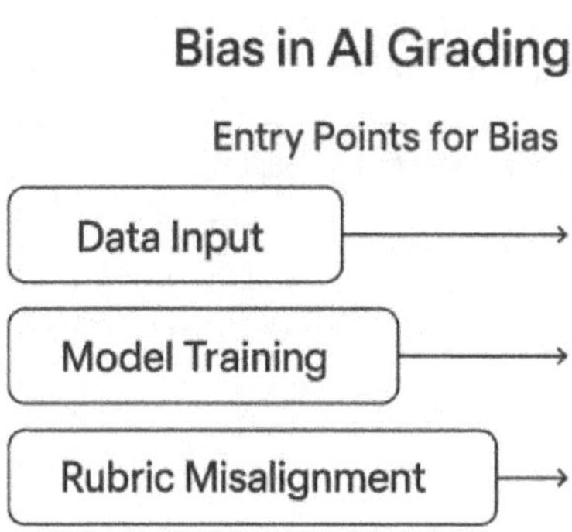

Workflow: Blended AI + Human Feedback Cycle

No AI model can replicate a teacher's insight. But with the right design, AI and humans can collaborate effectively. Here's a sample blended assessment workflow:

1. **Assignment Submission**: Students submit essays or quizzes via LMS
2. **AI First Pass**:
    - Grades auto-scored based on rubric
    - Feedback generated on structure, grammar, clarity
    - Plagiarism scan initiated
3. **Human Review**:
    - Teacher receives AI summary with highlighted flags
    - Final grade and feedback adjusted based on teacher input
4. **Student Feedback Released**:
    - Feedback shows both AI observations and teacher comments
    - Encourages transparency and trust

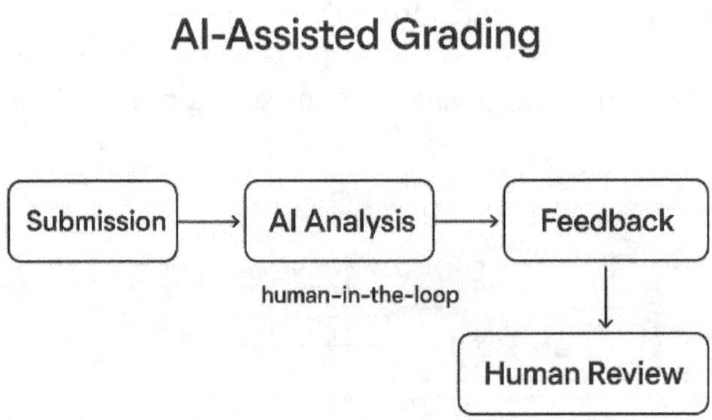

Real-World Example: District-Wide AI Grading Pilot

What Happened

A large U.S. school district partnered with an EdTech provider to test AI-assisted grading in high school English classes. Over one semester, the system graded over 100,000 essays using NLP models, with teachers reviewing 30% of submissions for quality assurance.

What Went Right or Wrong

Efficiency gains were clear: teachers reported saving 40% of their grading time. But initial feedback flagged several issues:

- Essays with unconventional formats were misjudged
- English learners' writing was disproportionately downgraded
- Teachers lacked confidence in the AI's scoring logic

In response, the district implemented mandatory teacher review for flagged essays and expanded rubric customization.

What We Learn from It

AI grading saves time—but only when trust is earned. Teachers must stay central to interpretation. Transparency and override capabilities are non-negotiable. The pilot also showed that teachers appreciated AI most *not* for final grades, but for helping identify who needed help, faster.

Tactical Best Practices for Educators and EdTech Leaders

- **Use AI to triage, not replace.** Let it sort submissions, but always keep final authority human.
- **Audit regularly.** Periodically check AI scores against teacher judgments to ensure alignment.
- **Explain to students.** If AI is used in grading, students should know how and why.
- **Keep rubrics transparent.** Let AI match your rubric—not the other way around.
- **Start small.** Pilot with low-stakes assessments before scaling to major grades.

Common Pitfalls to Avoid

- **Blind trust in AI scoring.** Even the best models make contextual mistakes.
- **Neglecting teacher input.** Teachers need time to review AI output—don't turn them into rubber stamps.
- **Poor feedback integration.** If AI and teacher feedback conflict or confuse, students disengage.
- **Ignoring student voice.** Students should have a way to appeal or clarify when AI misjudges their work.

Checklist: Building a Responsible AI Grading System

- Select tools with customizable rubrics and transparency features
- Train teachers in AI interpretation, not just tool use
- Define thresholds for human override or review
- Audit bias across demographics and writing styles
- Ensure students know how their work is assessed
- Integrate feedback loops for continuous improvement

Conclusion

AI-powered assessment is not about replacing the red pen—it's about using it smarter. When grading becomes faster, more consistent, and data-rich, educators get to spend more time doing what matters: teaching, mentoring, and inspiring. But none of that works without trust, transparency, and a human in the loop. Schools that embrace AI wisely don't automate grading—they transform it.

Next Steps

Assessment is only one part of the learning equation. What about students with learning differences, disabilities, or alternative communication needs? In **Chapter 5: AI in Special Education and Accessibility**, we explore how technology is empowering neurodiverse learners, breaking down barriers, and personalizing support in ways never before possible.

Chapter 5: AI in Special Education and Accessibility

For millions of students, learning isn't just about comprehension—it's about access. Traditional classrooms often overlook the needs of neurodiverse learners, non-verbal students, and those with cognitive or physical disabilities. These students face barriers that aren't about motivation or intelligence, but about how information is delivered, processed, and expressed.

Artificial intelligence is quietly transforming this reality. Today, AI tools can transcribe spoken words into text, read documents aloud, detect emotional cues, and adapt interfaces to suit each learner's needs. This is not a side benefit of educational AI—it's one of its most urgent and human-centered applications. In this chapter, we examine how AI is bridging the accessibility gap, equipping educators to support every learner, and turning personalized learning into a human right, not a privilege.

From Accommodation to Empowerment

Historically, accessibility in education has been reactive. Support often came after diagnosis, after struggle, and after paperwork. But AI flips that timeline. It allows real-time adaptation and proactive support—quietly and unobtrusively, embedded in the tools students already use.

Speech-to-Text and Text-to-Speech

For students with dyslexia, auditory processing issues, or physical impairments that limit typing, these tools open doors. AI-driven systems now offer:

- **Live captions** during lectures
- **Instant voice-to-text** transcription for assignments
- **Natural voice synthesis** to read documents aloud

Unlike older versions, today's tools are context-aware and multilingual, improving comprehension while preserving dignity.

Emotion-Aware Tutoring Bots

AI systems can now detect frustration, confusion, or disengagement through voice tone, typing speed, or facial expression. These emotion-aware bots adjust their responses accordingly—slowing down, simplifying language, or suggesting breaks.

Caution is warranted, of course. Emotional inference is still an imperfect science. But when used to support—not surveil—emotion-aware tools help educators respond to needs they might otherwise miss.

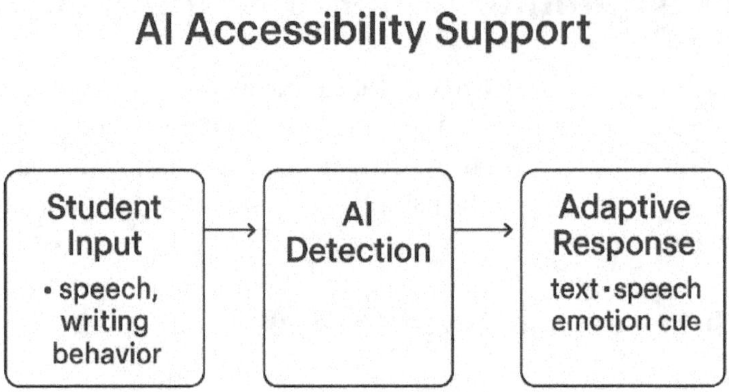

Empowering Neurodiverse and Non-Verbal Learners

Neurodiversity includes conditions like ADHD, autism spectrum disorder, dyscalculia, and more. Each presents unique learning profiles that traditional classrooms rarely accommodate fully. AI, by contrast, can tailor content and interaction modes in real time.

Tailored Interfaces and Pacing

AI systems can detect when a student loses focus, needs repetition, or benefits from gamified prompts. They can slow down or chunk content automatically. For example:

- Students with ADHD may get shorter bursts of content followed by micro-rewards
- Autistic learners may engage better with predictable, structured lesson formats

Visual and Non-Verbal Expression Tools

For non-verbal or minimally verbal students, AI unlocks expression. Tools can convert gestures, images, or gaze patterns into words or commands. Combined with alternative communication devices (AACs), students can engage in class discussions, complete assignments, and ask for help independently.

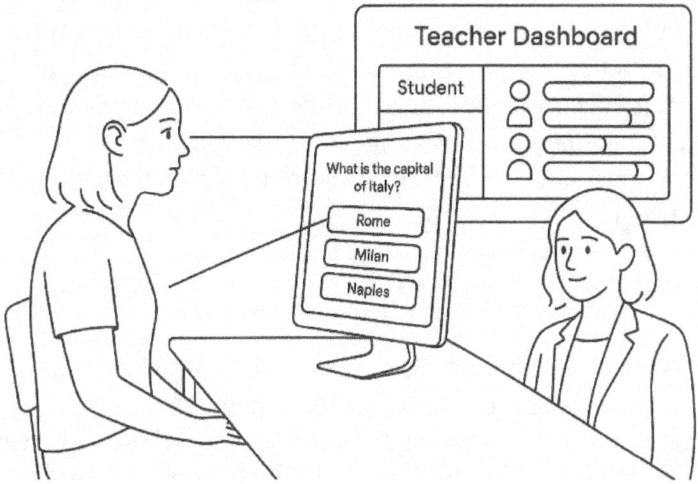

Real-World Example: Microsoft's Accessibility AI Tools

What Happened

Microsoft launched two tools that exemplify AI in accessibility: **Immersive Reader** and **Seeing AI**.

Immersive Reader uses AI to break down reading barriers. It can:

- Highlight parts of speech in different colors
- Adjust line spacing and font for dyslexic readers
- Read text aloud in real time

Seeing AI is designed for students with visual impairments. It narrates the world through a smartphone camera—reading documents, identifying objects, even recognizing emotions on faces.

These tools were integrated into classrooms globally, including in special education programs in the U.S., U.K., and India.

What Went Right or Wrong

Adoption was smooth where devices and internet access were reliable. Teachers reported higher engagement, and students showed more confidence in completing reading tasks independently. However, schools without strong tech infrastructure faced barriers—especially in rural or underfunded districts. Teacher training also varied, affecting usage depth.

What We Learn from It

The tools work—if the ecosystem supports them. Accessibility is not just about AI. It's about policy, training, bandwidth, and leadership commitment. Microsoft's approach proves that when AI is designed with empathy and inclusivity, it can radically expand what's possible for students who were once underserved.

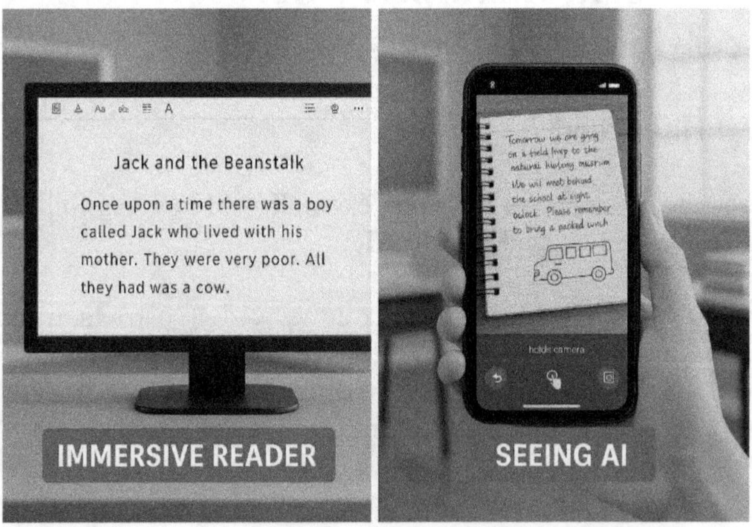

Tactical Best Practices for Schools and Developers

- **Design for inclusion first.** Don't retrofit accessibility—build it in from the beginning.
- **Ensure multimodal learning.** Offer text, audio, visual, and interactive paths simultaneously.
- **Involve real users.** Test tools with neurodiverse and disabled students during development.
- **Support teacher onboarding.** Provide clear use cases, guides, and live support.
- **Pair tech with human aides.** AI is most powerful when it extends—not replaces—human support.

Common Pitfalls to Avoid

- **Overgeneralizing disabilities.** "Accessibility" is not one feature—tailor to specific learner types.
- **Neglecting data privacy.** Emotion-aware tools must store and process data ethically.
- **Assuming tech alone solves inequity.** Infrastructure, funding, and training are essential.
- **Failing to test across contexts.** What works in one classroom may fail in another without adaptation.

Checklist: Building Inclusive Classrooms with AI

- Audit current barriers for neurodiverse and disabled students
- Identify where AI tools can assist (reading, speech, emotion, mobility)
- Ensure device access and stable internet connections
- Select tools that integrate with existing platforms (e.g., LMS)
- Train staff in accessibility-first teaching with AI
- Involve students and parents in feedback and tool selection

Conclusion

AI can't fix every barrier in education—but it can dismantle some of the hardest ones. When designed with empathy and deployed with purpose, AI becomes an amplifier of human potential. For learners once left behind, it offers a voice, a guide, and a bridge to full participation. That's not innovation for its own sake—it's education at its most just and powerful.

Next Steps

Technology is changing classrooms—but it's also changing teachers. What happens when AI takes over tasks that once defined the profession? In **Chapter 6: Redefining the Teacher's Role in an AI World**, we'll explore how educators are evolving into coaches, data translators, and emotional anchors—and what that means for training, identity, and future-ready teaching.

Chapter 6: Redefining the Teacher's Role in an AI World

For generations, the teacher stood at the center of the classroom as the primary source of knowledge. The chalkboard was their stage, the textbook their script, and the lecture their delivery. But in today's AI-enabled classrooms, knowledge is no longer scarce—and certainly no longer gated behind a single figure at the front of the room.

Artificial intelligence is reshaping not just how students learn, but how teachers teach. As AI takes over repetitive grading, real-time diagnostics, and personalized instruction delivery, the teacher's role is evolving. But this is not a story of replacement—it's a story of reinvention. In this chapter, we explore how educators are becoming coaches, mentors, and strategic learning designers. And we'll see how, in places like Singapore, this shift is already redefining the future of teaching.

From Knowledge Dispenser to Learning Architect

In AI-supported classrooms, students can access information anytime. But information isn't understanding. Students still need help navigating complexity, evaluating sources, and building confidence. That's where the teacher steps in—not to *deliver* content, but to *orchestrate* the learning experience.

New Core Roles for the AI-Era Teacher

- **Learning Coach**: Guiding students to reflect on their learning styles, set goals, and build habits
- **Feedback Strategist**: Interpreting AI-generated insights and giving targeted, timely feedback
- **Trust Builder**: Humanizing the tech experience, ensuring students feel seen and supported
- **Ethics Steward**: Helping students question, critique, and responsibly use AI tools

Teaching in an AI-Rich Environment

Instead of preparing the same lesson 5 times a day, teachers now:

- Monitor dashboards to spot struggling students in real time
- Adjust groupings based on skill mastery from adaptive platforms
- Use class time for collaboration, discussion, and higher-order thinking

Traditional Teacher

Class Preparation

- Prepare lesson materials
- Plan instructional activities

Instruction

- Deliver lesson
- Provide assistance

Grading

- Review and grade assignments
- Record grades

Assessment

- Create assesssments
- Evaluate student performance

AI-Enabled Teacher

Class Preparation

- Set up lesson framework
- Review AI-generated materials

Instruction

- Guide lesson
- Monitor AI-driven activities
- Provide targeted support

Grading

- Validate AI-generated grades
- Review flagged work

Administrative Tasks

- Review AI-generated reports
- Communication with parents

Training Teachers to Work With AI, Not Fear It

Fear of obsolescence is real—and understandable. But the greatest threat to the teaching profession isn't AI—it's resisting its integration. To make the shift, teachers need more than tools. They need training, support, and a mindset shift.

The Professional Development Gap

Too many schools adopt AI platforms without equipping teachers to use them effectively. The result? Frustration, underuse, or worse—complete rejection.

Principles for Empowering Teacher Training

- **Start with the "why."** Connect AI tools to teaching goals—not administrative ones
- **Demystify the tech.** Explain what the AI is doing (and not doing) under the hood

- **Focus on interpretation.** Teach how to read and act on AI-generated insights
- **Model blended roles.** Use coaching and role-play to practice the new educator identity
- **Create collaborative pilots.** Let teachers co-lead AI integration, not just follow it

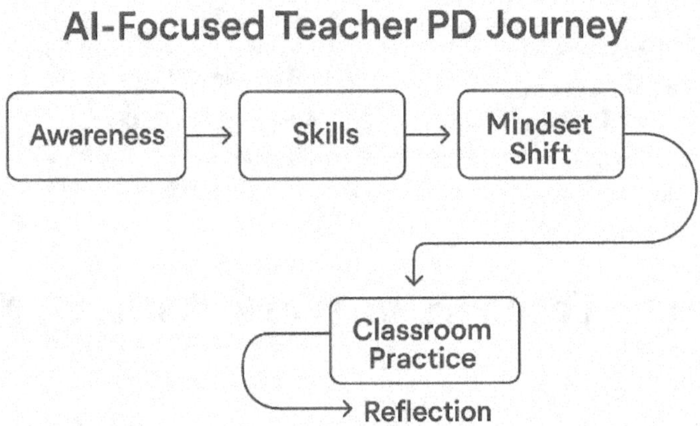

Real-World Example: Teacher Transformation in Singapore

What Happened

In 2021, Singapore's Ministry of Education began a structured rollout of AI-enhanced tools across pilot secondary schools. Teachers were introduced to adaptive learning platforms, predictive analytics dashboards, and feedback automation engines.

What Went Right or Wrong

The program's success hinged on intensive training—not just in using tools, but in rethinking roles. Teachers participated in design sprints with tech developers, co-created lesson templates, and reviewed student dashboards collaboratively.

Results included:

- Increased student engagement in self-paced modules
- Faster intervention for students at risk of falling behind
- Higher teacher satisfaction due to reduced grading load and deeper coaching relationships

Challenges? Initial anxiety and pushback were common. But peer mentoring and visible leadership buy-in helped shift the culture.

What We Learn from It

Teacher buy-in isn't about tech proficiency—it's about ownership and identity. Singapore's pilot shows that when teachers are invited to lead AI integration, not just respond to it, they don't resist change—they drive it.

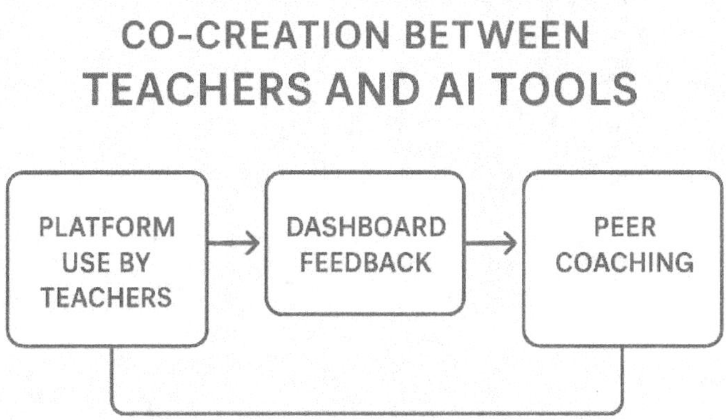

Tactical Best Practices for School Leaders and Teacher Trainers

- **Engage early adopters.** Let tech-savvy teachers lead pilot groups and train peers
- **Build in reflection time.** Teachers need structured time to evaluate what AI insights mean
- **Link AI use to outcomes.** Show how tools impact student success, not just speed
- **Respect teacher expertise.** Position AI as an assistant, not a replacement
- **Celebrate new roles.** Honor the shift from "lecturer" to "learning designer"

Common Pitfalls to Avoid

- **Pushing AI as mandatory without vision.** This breeds resentment and minimal compliance
- **Underestimating emotional labor.** Changing identity takes time and trust
- **Overloading with tools.** Focus on a few platforms that solve real problems
- **Leaving ethics out of the conversation.** Teachers need clarity on student data use and boundaries

Checklist: Supporting the Teacher Role in an AI World

- Clarify how AI supports—not replaces—teacher responsibilities
- Offer tiered training (basic use, data interpretation, ethical use)
- Create space for teacher feedback on tools and data
- Recognize and reward new forms of instructional leadership
- Build mentorship networks for sustained peer support
- Make time for co-planning with AI dashboards and insights

Conclusion

AI is changing what it means to teach—but it isn't diminishing the role of educators. It's elevating it. Teachers are becoming more strategic, more relational, and more indispensable than ever. The future of teaching isn't about coding or automation—it's about connection, insight, and adaptability. In the age of AI, the teacher's superpower is not what they know, but how they help others learn.

Next Steps

Teaching evolves—and so do the environments where learning happens. In **Chapter 7: Smart Classrooms and the Rise of Learning Analytics**, we'll dive into the sensors, systems, and platforms reshaping the physical and digital classroom. From real-time feedback loops to predictive analytics, we'll explore how data is helping educators prevent dropout, boost engagement, and design smarter learning spaces.

Chapter 7: Smart Classrooms and the Rise of Learning Analytics

Step into a modern classroom today, and you may see more than whiteboards and worksheets. You might see sensors tracking engagement, smartboards guiding collaborative lessons, or dashboards surfacing insights in real time. Beneath this increasingly intelligent infrastructure lies a powerful idea: what if we could understand, in real time, *how* students are learning—not just what they've memorized?

Smart classrooms are making that vision real. They combine AI with learning analytics to turn passive environments into responsive ones. Data becomes a feedback loop, not just an archive. And for teachers, that means actionable insight into student attention, participation, and risk—before it's too late to intervene.

This chapter explores how smart technology is reshaping educational spaces, how predictive analytics is helping schools tackle dropout and disengagement, and how tools like Classcraft, BrightBytes, and Edsby are making these capabilities practical and scalable.

What Makes a Classroom "Smart"?

A smart classroom doesn't mean screens on every wall or futuristic gadgets for the sake of it. It means learning environments where digital tools *listen*, *interpret*, and *respond*—all while supporting the human connections that matter most.

Core Technologies in Smart Classrooms

- **Interactive Smartboards**: Facilitate real-time collaboration, dynamic content delivery, and multimodal instruction
- **Sensor-Based Feedback**: Cameras and sensors detect student motion, voice levels, and even facial expressions to assess engagement
- **Wearables & Input Devices**: Some pilots use wristbands or clickers to track participation or stress signals
- **Learning Management Systems (LMS) + AI Dashboards**: Pull behavioral and performance data into unified views for teachers

These systems work together to create real-time feedback loops that help teachers adjust instruction on the fly.

Real-Time Feedback and Predictive Power

The power of smart classrooms isn't in the hardware—it's in the analytics. AI processes the constant stream of data into patterns and predictions. Teachers can then act with foresight, not just hindsight.

Real-Time Feedback Loops

- **Example**: A teacher receives a dashboard alert when average attention span dips, prompting an activity switch
- **Example**: Engagement sensors show that students are interacting less with peer group prompts, triggering a classroom reconfiguration

This is where data becomes teaching fuel—not just administrative reporting.

Predictive Analytics in Action

AI models now detect early signals of disengagement or dropout risk, such as:

- Consistent late logins to virtual classes
- Sudden dips in formative assessment scores
- Lack of interaction in collaborative tools

Predictive models don't just flag problems—they can suggest interventions, such as targeted outreach, mentoring, or adjustments to pacing.

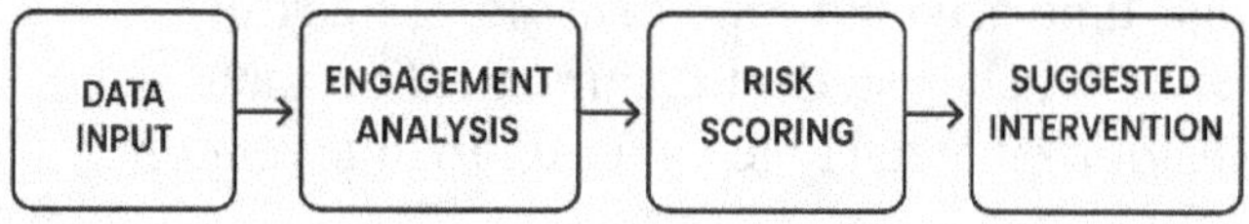

Tools Leading the Movement

Classcraft

A gamified classroom engagement platform. Classcraft turns participation into points and collaboration into quests, motivating students while feeding real-time data to teachers.

- Tracks social-emotional metrics
- Flags disengagement trends
- Encourages teamwork through game mechanics

BrightBytes

Designed for district-level insight. It aggregates data across systems—grades, attendance, engagement metrics—and turns it into visual dashboards that help administrators:

- Identify at-risk student populations
- Optimize tech investments
- Support equity initiatives

Edsby

A next-gen LMS with deep analytics baked in. Edsby provides:

- Real-time academic and behavioral tracking
- Parent-teacher-student communication tools
- Customizable data views for early intervention

Classcraft	BrightBytes	Edsby
USE CASES Behavior management Motivation	**USE TYPES** Data analytics Decision support	**USE CASES** Communication Engagement
USER TYPES Teachers Students	**USER TYPES** Administrators District leaders	**OUTCOMES** Teachers Parents Students
OUTCOMES Improved classroom behavior	**OUTCOMES** Informed decision-making	**OUTCOMES** Stronger school community

Real-World Example: District-Wide Engagement Monitoring

What Happened

A mid-sized district in Canada implemented BrightBytes to improve student retention. The goal was to combine attendance, test performance, and behavioral data to proactively identify dropouts before they happened.

What Went Right or Wrong

The system identified 78 high-risk students within two months—many of whom had never been flagged through traditional methods. Counselors used the insights to initiate early outreach, resulting in a 35% reduction in mid-year withdrawals.

However, some teachers felt overwhelmed by "dashboard fatigue" and struggled to interpret the flood of data. Leadership responded by streamlining the interface and integrating training sessions into PD days.

What We Learn from It

Smart classrooms generate *actionable insight*—but only if that insight is digestible and matched with the capacity to act. Technology must simplify, not complicate, the teacher's mission.

Tactical Best Practices for Leaders and Developers

- **Focus on usefulness, not novelty.** Choose tech that solves *specific* problems, not just impressive demos.
- **Streamline dashboards.** Teachers should see what matters—fast.
- **Link metrics to interventions.** Show what to *do* with each data point.
- **Train in small groups.** Use coaching cohorts to build confidence in reading and responding to analytics.
- **Guard against over-surveillance.** Transparency and student trust are essential—never track without consent.

Common Pitfalls to Avoid

- **Too much data, not enough context.** Data without strategy leads to overwhelm.
- **Ignoring privacy safeguards.** Sensor-based classrooms must comply with legal and ethical norms.
- **Treating all students the same.** Predictive tools must adjust for diverse learners—not apply blanket formulas.
- **Assuming tech equals engagement.** Tools help—but teacher relationship still drives motivation.

Checklist: Building a Smart, Data-Driven Classroom

- Identify core instructional challenges you want tech to solve
- Choose platforms that integrate across tools (LMS, grading, behavior)
- Define key performance indicators for engagement and progress
- Train staff in data literacy and feedback response
- Establish clear policies for data privacy and usage transparency
- Pilot with a small group before school-wide rollout

Conclusion

Smart classrooms are not about turning schools into labs—they're about making them more human, more responsive, and more effective. When data helps teachers spot needs early, adapt instruction quickly, and engage students more deeply, it's not just tech innovation—it's educational equity in action.

Next Steps

But insight without ethics can cause harm. As data becomes more powerful, so must our responsibility. In **Chapter 8: The Ethical AI Classroom**, we'll unpack the issues of privacy, consent, and fairness—and show how schools can build digital citizenship into every AI-powered lesson. You'll also get our Ethics Checklist infographic for schools ready to lead.

Chapter 8: The Ethical AI Classroom

Smart technology in schools brings incredible promise—but without a solid ethical foundation, that promise can quickly turn into a problem. As AI systems make decisions about how students learn, how they're assessed, and what interventions they receive, the stakes grow higher. We're no longer talking about theoretical risks—we're talking about the trust of students, the privacy of families, and the integrity of the education system itself.

The ethical AI classroom is not just a technical challenge—it's a cultural shift. It demands that educators, developers, and policymakers ask harder questions, design with care, and teach digital responsibility alongside digital skills. This chapter explores the essential ethical pillars—privacy, consent, fairness, and transparency—while offering a framework for building a curriculum of digital citizenship. We also introduce a practical tool for school leaders: the AI Bill of Rights for Schools.

Why Ethics Can't Be an Afterthought

AI systems are designed to optimize. But what they optimize—how, for whom, and under what assumptions—has ethical consequences. An algorithm trained to maximize test scores might favor rigid drill-and-kill learning. One that identifies "at-risk" students might encode racial or socioeconomic bias.

Ethics must be built in from the start. That means involving educators in tool selection, demanding transparency from vendors, and teaching students not just to *use* AI—but to *question* it.

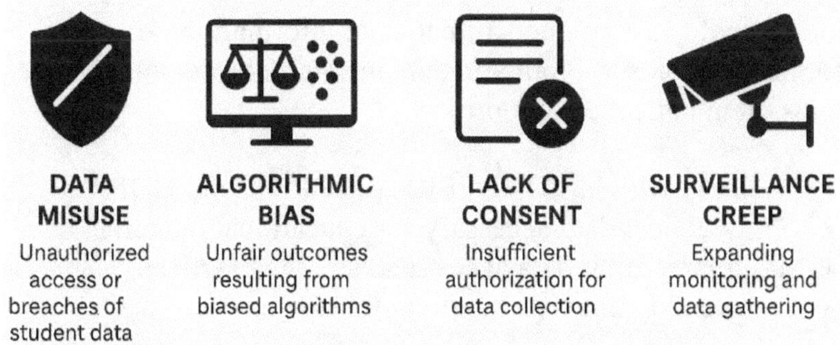

Four Core Pillars of Ethical AI Use in Schools

1. Consent and Transparency

Students and families must know when AI is being used, how it's making decisions, and what data is being collected. Opt-in policies are rare—but they should be standard for sensitive data collection.

- Always disclose when AI tools are being used in grading, behavior tracking, or predictive analytics
- Use plain language to explain tool functions and limitations
- Offer opt-outs for non-critical AI features

2. Data Privacy

Schools handle vast amounts of personal information—from performance scores to biometric data in smart classrooms. AI systems often collect even more.

- Comply with laws like FERPA, COPPA, and GDPR
- Only collect data necessary for educational outcomes
- Regularly audit data access and storage practices
- Vet vendors for data handling transparency

3. Fairness and Bias Prevention

AI must not reinforce inequality. Yet many systems are trained on biased data that favors majority norms.

- Regularly test AI outputs for differential outcomes by race, gender, language, and ability
- Customize tools to reflect local cultures and pedagogies
- Include diverse educators in tool evaluation and implementation

4. Explainability and Accountability

Teachers and students must be able to understand *why* an AI made a decision. “Black box” models with no transparency undermine trust.

- Choose tools that offer explainable AI (XAI) features
- Provide educators with clear rationale for AI-generated scores or alerts
- Allow human override on any AI-based action

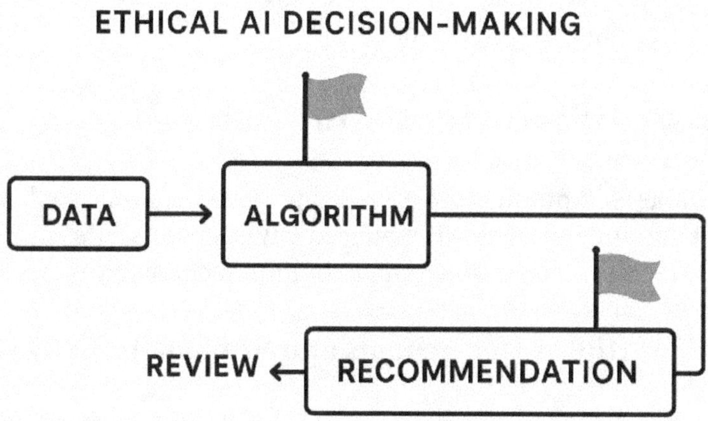

Building Digital Citizenship into the Curriculum

Teaching AI ethics shouldn’t be reserved for computer science electives. Every student needs to understand the tools shaping their education.

Core Concepts for K–12 AI Literacy

- **What AI is and isn't**: Clarify the limits of algorithmic intelligence
- **How data is used**: Show how behavior online shapes recommendations and assessments
- **Bias in systems**: Use examples to highlight unintentional discrimination
- **Questioning AI authority**: Teach students to ask "why" and "who benefits?"

Digital citizenship today must include *algorithmic awareness*—the ability to critique, not just comply.

The AI Bill of Rights for Schools

This framework outlines the essential protections every student and teacher should expect in AI-enhanced environments. It's a declaration of digital dignity and a tool for accountability.

AI Bill of Rights (for Schools and Students)

1. **The Right to Know** when AI is used and how it affects learning or evaluation
2. **The Right to Consent** to the collection and use of personal data beyond essential functions
3. **The Right to Opt Out** of non-essential AI-driven monitoring or recommendation systems
4. **The Right to Human Review** of any AI-generated assessment, prediction, or disciplinary flag
5. **The Right to Understand** how AI decisions are made, in plain language
6. **The Right to Equal Treatment**, regardless of background or learning profile
7. **The Right to Challenge** automated decisions and request corrections

8. **The Right to Data Security**, with protection against misuse, leaks, or overreach
9. **The Right to Learn About AI**, including its ethical use and limitations
10. **The Right to Be More Than Data**, recognizing students as full human beings, not just metrics

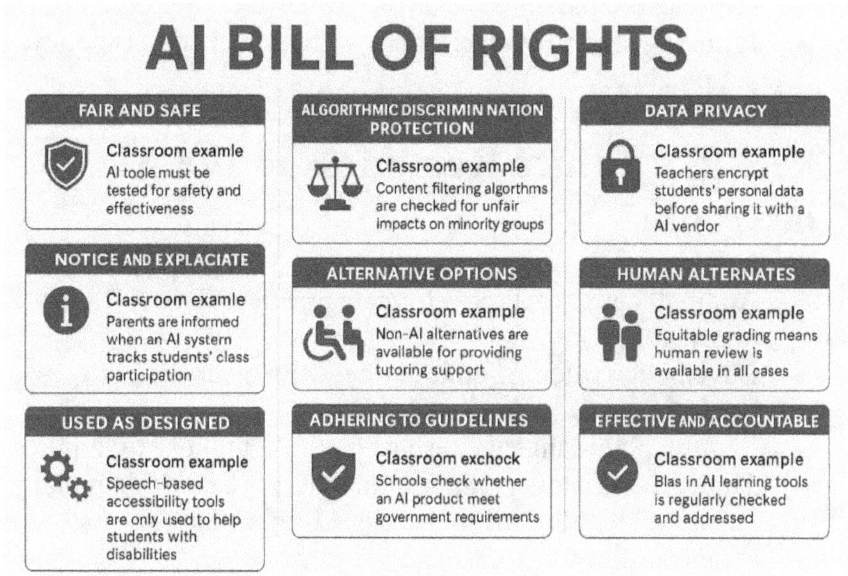

Tactical Best Practices for School Leaders and EdTech Teams

- **Create an AI ethics committee.** Include educators, students, IT leads, and parents
- **Mandate transparency from vendors.** Don't adopt tools without explainable features
- **Build ethical review into procurement.** Evaluate not just functionality, but fairness
- **Train staff in ethical data literacy.** Don't assume teachers understand algorithmic risk
- **Involve students in the conversation.** Let them help shape digital norms

Common Pitfalls to Avoid

- **Relying on vendor promises.** "Trust us" is not an audit trail
- **Skipping ethics because it's "complicated."** Complexity is not an excuse for inaction
- **Over-surveilling in the name of safety.** Monitor with purpose, not paranoia
- **Ignoring student voice.** Ethics without inclusion is policy, not practice

Checklist: Ethics Readiness in the AI Classroom

- Audit all current AI tools for data practices, bias risk, and transparency
- Develop a written AI ethics policy with clear student protections
- Require plain-language disclosure of AI tool use to families
- Train all educators in algorithmic literacy and explainability
- Create student forums to discuss AI rights and responsibilities
- Use the AI Bill of Rights as a checklist before adopting any new tool

Conclusion

Ethics isn't a layer we sprinkle on top of AI—it's the structure underneath. Without consent, fairness, and transparency, smart systems become surveillance systems. But with the right foundations, AI can enhance—not erode—human dignity in schools. The ethical classroom is a safe, inclusive, and empowering space for every student, guided by tools that serve learning, not just tracking.

Next Steps

AI is now in every classroom conversation—and no tool is more hotly debated than ChatGPT. In **Chapter 9: ChatGPT in Schools — Use It or Block It?**, we dive into the real risks and real opportunities behind this transformative tool. You'll get a prompt library by grade and subject, plus a practical policy guide for principals looking to lead with clarity.

Chapter 9: ChatGPT in Schools — Use It or Block It?

Few technologies have sparked more heated debate in education than ChatGPT. Launched with the promise of making information more accessible and language-based tasks easier, it quickly became both a revolutionary classroom tool and a source of deep concern. Some districts rushed to ban it; others embraced it as a new literacy frontier. Parents worried about cheating. Teachers asked whether writing skills would suffer. Students were already using it—quietly, curiously, and, in some cases, strategically.

The core question isn't whether ChatGPT is "good" or "bad." It's whether schools can guide its use thoughtfully. The truth is: this tool is already here, and students are already engaging with it. What matters now is whether educators choose to block it blindly—or harness it responsibly.

In this chapter, we dissect the real risks, explore safe and structured educational use cases, and offer a policy blueprint for school leaders. You'll also find a curated classroom prompt library by grade and subject—designed not just to use ChatGPT, but to teach students to *think with it*, *challenge it*, and *learn through it*.

The Debate: Blocker vs. Innovator

ChatGPT's rise hit many schools like a tidal wave. Some immediately blocked access on school networks, citing academic dishonesty, safety concerns, or policy gaps. Others leaned in, experimenting with writing support, tutoring, and creative projects.

Common Fears

- **Cheating on essays or assignments**
- **Dependence on AI over critical thinking**
- **Exposure to inappropriate or unvetted content**
- **Loss of traditional writing skills**

Missed Opportunities

- **Real-time feedback and scaffolding for struggling learners**
- **Support for English learners and neurodiverse students**
- **Creative ideation and brainstorming help**
- **Metacognitive growth through tool critique and comparison**

The tension boils down to this: Are we preparing students to navigate AI responsibly—or pretending they won't use it?

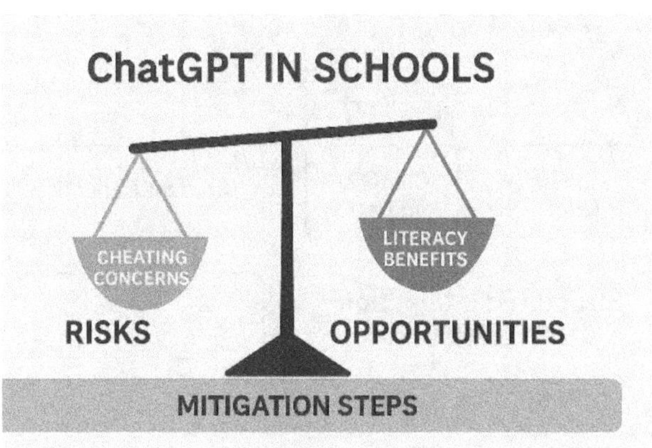

Safe, Structured Ways to Use ChatGPT in the Classroom

When used within clear boundaries, ChatGPT becomes a powerful tool—not just for content generation, but for critical thinking and digital literacy.

Pedagogically Aligned Use Cases

- **Socratic Prompts**: Ask ChatGPT to play the role of a philosopher, scientist, or historical figure for a structured dialogue
- **Revision Assistant**: Have students draft essays, then use ChatGPT to suggest improvements—and defend or reject those suggestions
- **STEM Explanations**: Let ChatGPT explain a concept (e.g., Newton's Laws) in three different ways, and ask students to compare accuracy and clarity
- **Idea Expansion**: Use prompts like "Give me three angles to explore the theme of resilience in this novel" to support brainstorming
- **Vocabulary Builder**: Ask for contextual definitions and example sentences, then have students rewrite or improve them

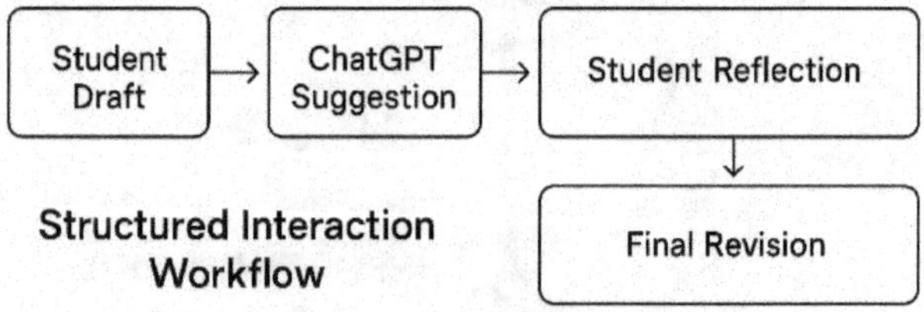

Classroom Prompt Library (By Grade Level and Subject)

A selection of vetted, educator-approved prompts to guide safe and meaningful use.

Elementary (Grades 3–5)

ELA: "Write a short story about a character who learns to be brave. Then, explain the lesson they learned."
Science: "Explain the water cycle in three steps, like you're talking to a friend."
Social Studies: "Pretend you are a child living in ancient Egypt. Describe your day."

Middle School (Grades 6–8)

ELA: "List three possible themes in this book, then give examples from the text."
Math: "Explain how to solve a linear equation. What are common mistakes?"
Science: "Debate: Should we colonize Mars? Give two arguments for and two against."

High School (Grades 9–12)

ELA: "Analyze the tone of this poem. How does word choice shape it?"
History: "Write a dialogue between two historians who disagree about the causes of World War I."
STEM: "Break down the concept of entropy in three levels: beginner, intermediate, advanced."

Bonus Prompts:

- "What's a misconception about this topic? Why do people believe it?"
- "Play devil's advocate on this issue. What's the strongest counterargument?"

CLASSROOM PROMPTS BY SUBJECT AND GRADE

PROMPT	LEARNING GOAL	CAUTION
English Language Arts (Grade 5) Write a letter from the perspective of a historical figure in your book.	Develop narrative writing skills	Verify historical accuracy of the content
Social Studies (Grade 7) Explain how supply and demand affect prices.	Understand economic concepts	Check for oversimplification or bias
Science (Grade 4) What are the steps of the water cycle?	Recall scientific processes	Ensure accurate and complete information
Mathematics (Grade 8) Solve this equation and provide the steps: 3x + 7 = 2x + 10	Improve algebraic problem-solving	Watch for errors in the solution
	Explore artistic techniques	Encourage originality and creative thinking

Principal's Guide to Writing a ChatGPT Policy

ChatGPT policy isn't about blanket bans or unchecked freedom—it's about clarity. The best school policies position the tool as *optional, guided, and transparent*.

Key Policy Elements

- **Purpose Statement**: Define why the tool is being considered (literacy support, inquiry, etc.)
- **Approved Use Cases**: Identify which assignments or grade levels allow ChatGPT use
- **Student Accountability**: Require disclosure of ChatGPT use in submissions (e.g., footnote, AI use form)
- **Teacher Discretion**: Allow educators to define when ChatGPT is or isn't appropriate in their classrooms
- **Ethics and Literacy Mandate**: Require digital literacy instruction on AI limits and bias
- **Data Privacy Guidelines**: Clarify what data is shared and how students are protected

ChatGPT Use Policy

Purpose

This policy outlines proper use of ChatGPT as an educational tool and encourages responsible use.

Scope

This policy applies schoolwide to both teachers and students.

Teacher Guidance

- Use ChatGPT ssull-be supplement, not replace, traditional instruction
- Review chatGPT outputs for accuracy and alignment with educational gith educational goals
- Introduce students to ChatGPT's capabilities, and limitations

Student Rules

- Use ChatGPT only as directed by a teacher
- Not use ChatGPT to complete assignments wit permission
- Critically avaluate information provided by ChatGPT
- Not access ChatGPT during quizzes or tests
- Adhere to school's code of conduct when use using ChatGPT

Tactical Best Practices for Teachers and Leaders

- **Teach AI critique before AI use.** Start by asking: "How might this tool get things wrong?"
- **Set clear rules of engagement.** When is use allowed? When is it plagiarism?
- **Build reflection into the workflow.** Ask students to annotate, compare, or critique ChatGPT outputs.
- **Model responsible use.** Use it in lessons visibly and transparently.
- **Don't over-rely.** ChatGPT should scaffold learning—not replace thinking.

Common Pitfalls to Avoid

- **Treating ChatGPT as a shortcut.** Without reflection, it undermines deeper learning.
- **Assuming accuracy.** Students must be taught to fact-check and cross-reference.
- **Using it for everything.** ChatGPT is one tool—not a replacement for books, teachers, or peers.
- **Lack of visibility.** Secretive or unregulated use erodes trust and accountability.

Checklist: Launching a School-Wide ChatGPT Strategy

- Survey teachers and students on current use and attitudes
- Define approved and restricted use cases by grade
- Develop a shared ethics and literacy framework for AI tools
- Pilot classroom prompts across subjects
- Create a visible reporting and feedback loop for challenges
- Update digital citizenship curriculum to include AI critique

Conclusion

The ChatGPT debate reveals a deeper truth: our role isn't to fear new tools—it's to lead their responsible integration. Blocking may seem safer, but it won't prepare students for the world they're entering. Teaching them to *use* ChatGPT critically, ethically, and creatively? That's real preparation for the age of AI.

Next Steps

AI is changing how students think—but it's also starting to monitor *how they feel.* In **Chapter 10: AI and Student Mental Health Monitoring**, we examine emotion AI, burnout alerts, and the fine line between help and overreach. We'll look at Stanford's pilot program—and the red lines every school should draw.

Chapter 10: AI and Student Mental Health Monitoring

Mental health is no longer a side conversation in education—it's front and center. Schools are grappling with rising anxiety, burnout, and disengagement among students, compounded by post-pandemic challenges, academic pressure, and social media saturation. At the same time, resources for counselors and school psychologists are stretched dangerously thin.

Enter AI: tools that promise to detect emotional distress early, identify patterns of disengagement, and even alert staff to signs of depression or burnout before a student ever says a word. From sentiment analysis in essays to facial expression monitoring, a wave of "emotion AI" and well-being platforms is being introduced to help schools intervene sooner.

But there's a fine line between supporting students and surveilling them. This chapter explores the promise and peril of AI-based mental health monitoring in education, with a deep dive into Stanford's high-profile pilot, and clear red lines every school should draw to protect student autonomy.

Where AI Can Help: Early Detection and Scalable Support

Mental health issues often go unreported until they escalate. AI offers the potential to catch early signs that human staff may miss—especially in large, under-resourced schools.

Key Capabilities

- **Emotion Recognition**: AI tools analyze facial expressions, speech tone, and even typing rhythm to infer emotional states like stress or sadness.
- **Behavioral Analytics**: Platforms track changes in attendance, assignment submissions, screen time, and engagement as indicators of potential concern.
- **Burnout and Dropout Risk Alerts**: Predictive models combine academic and behavioral data to flag students who may be struggling silently.

These systems aim to supplement—not replace—human relationships. When used well, they help counselors focus limited time where it's needed most.

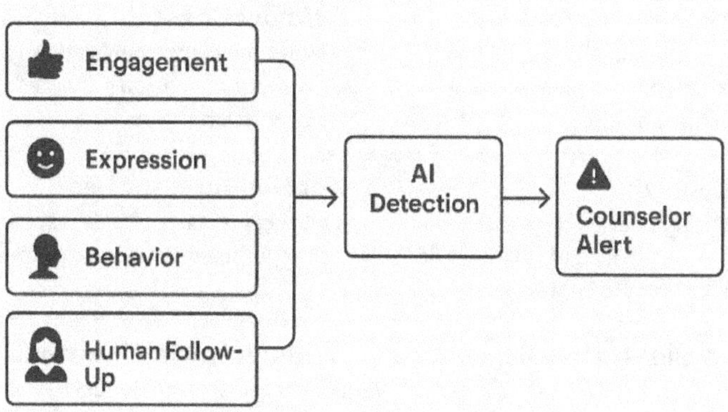

Where It Overreaches: Risks and Boundaries

The same tools that offer insight can also cross ethical lines. When AI is used without transparency, consent, or human judgment, the result is often fear, stigma, and loss of trust.

Top Concerns

- **Privacy Violations**: Monitoring students' emotional states through cameras or keystrokes can feel invasive.
- **Misinterpretation**: AI can mistake introversion or cultural communication styles for distress.
- **Over-Flagging**: Constant alerts can overwhelm staff or falsely pathologize normal adolescent behavior.
- **Stigmatization**: Being labeled as "at-risk" by a machine can follow a student through their records—and affect how they're treated.

The key distinction? AI *should alert*, not *diagnose*. It should guide human action, not replace it.

APPROPRIATE	INAPPROPRIATIE
With Informed Consent Using AI to support mental health after obtaining explicit consent from the individual	**Without Consent** Monitoring mental health through AI without the person's knowledge or permission
In Context Analyzing relevant data to provide mental health insights in a specific and appropriate context	**For Non-Relevant Use** Utilizing mental health data in contex or for purposes that are not pertinent
Alongside Human Support Employing AI as a tool to aid, not replace, mental health professionals	**Without Human Oversight** Relying solely on AI for decision-mking in mental health without professional intervention

Real-World Example: Stanford's AI Well-Being Pilot

What Happened

Stanford piloted an AI-driven student well-being platform across several departments. The system tracked attendance, LMS activity, and even the emotional tone of written reflections to detect signs of burnout or depression. Students received gentle nudges ("Would you like to talk to someone?") while staff received pattern-based alerts.

What Went Right or Wrong

The platform led to earlier outreach for dozens of students, with many expressing appreciation for the check-ins. Counselors reported that it helped them prioritize outreach and follow up more meaningfully.

However, some students expressed concern about being watched or judged based on writing tone. Others worried about being misunderstood or misflagged. The pilot was later revised to include:

- Explicit consent forms
- Transparent dashboards showing what was being tracked
- A review panel for flagged cases before any staff action

What We Learn from It

Even in high-trust environments like Stanford, students want control over how they're monitored. Successful systems make *support feel like support*—not surveillance. And no matter how good the algorithm, a human conversation must always come next.

Red Lines: Non-Negotiables in Mental Health AI

Red Line 1: No Surveillance Without Consent

Students must know what's being monitored, why, and how it will be used. Opt-in must be real and revocable.

Red Line 2: AI Never Replaces Human Judgment

Automated alerts should be triaged and interpreted by trained professionals—not trigger punitive action or automated messaging without context.

Red Line 3: Transparent Access to Records

Students should be able to view, challenge, or correct any mental health-related data being logged about them.

Red Line 4: Cultural Sensitivity Must Be Built In

Emotion detection models must be tested across cultures and neurotypes to avoid biased interpretations.

Red Line 5: Wellness ≠ Discipline

Mental health monitoring should be handled by counselors and wellness teams—not school discipline staff or administrators.

STUDENT AUTONOMY FIRST

- Don't infer emotions from facial expressions
- Don't make psychological profiles of students
- Don't personalize learning based on emotion
- Don't identify students by emotional state
- Don't use emotion data to make decisions

! AI use on emotion AI impliangment

Tactical Best Practices for Schools Considering Mental Health AI

- **Pilot with transparency**: Begin with opt-in programs and informed student-parent engagement
- **Build human response plans**: Every AI alert should link to a real human intervention pathway
- **Audit frequently**: Check for demographic bias and over-flagging in flagged cases
- **Create student advisory panels**: Let students shape the boundaries of well-being tech
- **Train staff in ethics**: Ensure that teachers and counselors understand what the AI sees—and doesn't see

Common Pitfalls to Avoid

- **Assuming more data = better outcomes**: Focus on *meaningful* signals, not just volume
- **Equating disengagement with distress**: Boredom and burnout are not always the same
- **Letting tech outpace policy**: Don't deploy tools faster than you can govern them
- **Treating students as subjects, not partners**: Ethical use begins with student voice

Checklist: Responsible AI Mental Health Use

- Clearly define the goals of monitoring (burnout, crisis prevention, etc.)
- Secure opt-in consent with revocation options
- Vet AI tools for cultural and neurodiversity awareness
- Build manual review and triage into all alert systems
- Involve students and counselors in system design
- Provide transparency into what data is collected and why

Conclusion

Mental health support is essential—but how we deliver it matters as much as *that* we deliver it. AI can help us listen more closely to students—but only if we listen with care, consent, and context. The future of well-being in schools isn't automated care—it's augmented care. And that begins with trust.

Next Steps

Student wellness is only one side of the system. In **Chapter 11: AI for School Operations and Administration**, we explore how AI is transforming the backend of education—from scheduling and budgeting to HR and procurement. You'll hear from principals, explore tools like IBM Watson, and learn how to free up time for what matters most: learning.

Chapter 11: AI for School Operations and Administration

Most of the attention around AI in education has focused on classrooms—adaptive learning, personalized tutoring, automated feedback. But behind every great learning environment is an administrative system that runs smoothly, allocates resources wisely, and empowers educators to focus on what matters: teaching.

For too long, school operations have been buried in paperwork, legacy systems, and time-intensive manual tasks. From building master schedules to processing purchase orders, these backend functions consume hours of staff time and strain already limited budgets. Now, AI is stepping in—not with flashy tools, but with deeply practical solutions.

This chapter explores how AI is transforming the business of running a school: scheduling, budgeting, HR, procurement, and beyond. We'll look at tools like IBM Watson and PowerSchool Predictive Suite, and hear directly from principals who've embraced automation to shift their focus from administration to instruction.

Where Schools Waste Time and Resources

Education leaders know the truth: administrative tasks are eating into instructional priorities. Principals spend more time troubleshooting logistics than observing classrooms. District leaders wrestle with reactive budgeting, clunky procurement, and incomplete data.

Key pain points include:

- **Manual scheduling conflicts** (teacher availability, room assignment, student course requests)
- **Budget overruns due to poor forecasting**
- **Inefficient hiring processes and HR paperwork**
- **Procurement delays for everything from tech to textbooks**

AI doesn't just streamline these processes—it brings a level of foresight and optimization that manual systems can't match.

Core Use Cases for AI in School Operations

1. Automated Scheduling

Tools powered by AI can generate optimized class schedules by balancing:

- Student course preferences
- Staff availability
- Room capacity
- Equity in teacher assignments

They resolve conflicts in minutes—something that used to take entire teams days to do manually.

2. Budget Forecasting and Optimization

AI-driven financial planning platforms analyze past spending, current allocations, and enrollment projections to:

- Suggest reallocations
- Flag anomalies
- Predict shortfalls before they happen

This helps schools make data-informed, forward-looking budget decisions.

3. Human Resources Automation

From resume screening to onboarding workflows, AI can:

- Pre-screen candidates based on skill and credential matches
- Auto-schedule interviews
- Handle routine employee inquiries via chatbots
- Surface retention risk indicators based on engagement or absenteeism patterns

4. Smart Procurement and Inventory

Predictive procurement systems learn from usage patterns and seasonal trends to:

- Recommend optimal order timing
- Alert when contracts are nearing expiration
- Prevent over-ordering or understocking supplies

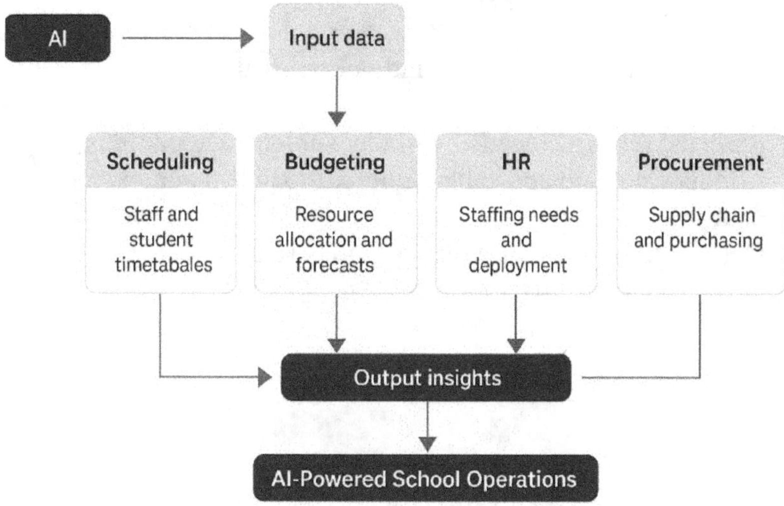

Tools Leading the Charge

IBM Watson for Education (Ops Module)

Watson offers a robust AI engine that integrates across financial systems, HR, and student data. It can:

- Predict enrollment trends
- Optimize workforce deployment
- Support school board reporting with automated data visualization

PowerSchool Predictive Suite

This platform combines academic and operational data to:

- Forecast resource needs by grade, subject, and campus
- Connect staffing and scheduling with student achievement data
- Deliver real-time alerts on anomalies (e.g., underspent grants or overbooked staff)

	IBM Watson	PowerSchool Predictive Suite
Features	• Machine learning • Natural language processing • Data analysis • Customizable mo-dels	• Student performance analysis • Risk assessment • Intervention suggestions • Attendance tracking
User Type	Businesses	Educational institutions
Operational Impact	• Enhances decis-ion-making • Improves process efficiency	• Supports student success • Reduces dropout rates

Principal Testimonials: Efficiency That Frees Up Time

Principal Andrea Morales, CA
"We used to spend six weeks building our master schedule. With AI assistance, we finished in four days—and it's more equitable than ever."

Principal James Koh, TX
"PowerSchool helped us reallocate $180,000 in unused budget line items to student tech access. I wouldn't have spotted it without the alerts."

Principal Leena Das, NY
"AI in HR flagged a potential retention issue based on absentee patterns—and helped us intervene early. That teacher is still with us."

These stories are more than anecdotes—they signal a shift in how schools are managed. When admin burden decreases, leadership impact increases.

Tactical Best Practices for AI-Driven School Operations

- **Start with a single high-impact domain.** Scheduling or budgeting are great entry points
- **Map existing workflows before integrating AI.** Understand current pain points clearly
- **Train admin teams alongside instructional staff.** Operational AI also requires digital fluency
- **Set goals beyond efficiency.** Focus on equity, transparency, and staff satisfaction
- **Build cross-functional teams.** Include finance, HR, IT, and leadership in planning and review

Common Pitfalls to Avoid

- **Expecting AI to fix broken systems.** Automating bad processes just makes them faster
- **Skipping staff onboarding.** Adoption fails when teams don't understand the "why" and "how"
- **Ignoring data hygiene.** AI outputs are only as good as the input—clean your systems first
- **Leaving teachers out of scheduling decisions.** Use AI to *assist*, not dictate

Checklist: Building AI-Ready School Operations

- Identify the top three time-draining admin processes
- Audit current data systems for quality and accessibility
- Pilot AI scheduling or budgeting with one department or school
- Create staff training plans for admin AI tools
- Evaluate vendor transparency and support options
- Measure impact by time saved, budget accuracy, and user satisfaction

Conclusion

AI in school operations isn't about cutting staff—it's about cutting the noise. When principals spend less time in spreadsheets and more time with students, everyone benefits. With the right tools and leadership, AI can turn schools into agile, data-smart organizations where every decision is anchored in clarity—not chaos.

Next Steps

Tools are powerful, but culture makes or breaks implementation. In **Chapter 12: Building an AI-Ready School Culture**, we'll look at how to cultivate buy-in, shift mindsets, and roll out professional development that sticks. Plus: your 12-month roadmap to sustainable, school-wide AI integration.

Chapter 12: Building an AI-Ready School Culture

No technology—no matter how powerful—succeeds without culture behind it. Schools that integrate AI successfully don't start with the tools; they start with trust, training, and a clear sense of purpose. AI adoption in education isn't just a technical initiative—it's a leadership challenge, a mindset shift, and a long-game investment in people.

Yet many schools get stuck at the same point: enthusiasm at the top, hesitation at the ground level. "We've always done it this way" becomes the quiet blocker of innovation. This chapter focuses on how to build a culture that's not only ready for AI, but ready to adapt, experiment, and grow. You'll find a professional development blueprint, real-world examples of pilot success, and a practical 12-month roadmap to bring your school into the AI era—at a sustainable pace.

Why Culture Eats Strategy (and Tech) for Breakfast

AI tools are only as effective as the people using them. Without cultural readiness, even the best systems end up abandoned, underused, or misaligned with student needs. Resistance isn't usually about the technology itself—it's about fear, fatigue, or lack of clarity.

Core Cultural Barriers to AI Adoption

- **Change fatigue**: "Another tool? Another training?"
- **Fear of being replaced**: Especially among veteran teachers
- **Lack of vision alignment**: Teachers unsure how AI supports pedagogy
- **No time to learn**: Packed schedules leave no room for exploration

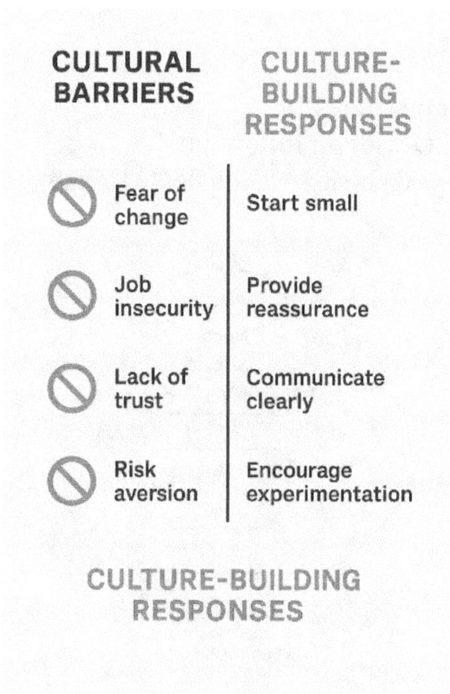

Training and Buy-In: Where True Adoption Begins

You can't mandate mindset shifts. Buy-in happens when people feel safe, informed, and included. That means building *with* your staff, not *for* them.

What Works

- **Pilot programs with teacher choice**: Let teachers opt in and co-design
- **Time-bound experiments**: Frame AI use as exploration, not permanent change
- **Visible leadership use**: When principals use dashboards and AI tools, others follow
- **Peer modeling**: Leverage early adopters as trainers and mentors

What Doesn't

- Tool-first mandates
- One-off PD with no follow-up
- Assuming "tech-savvy" equals "AI-ready"

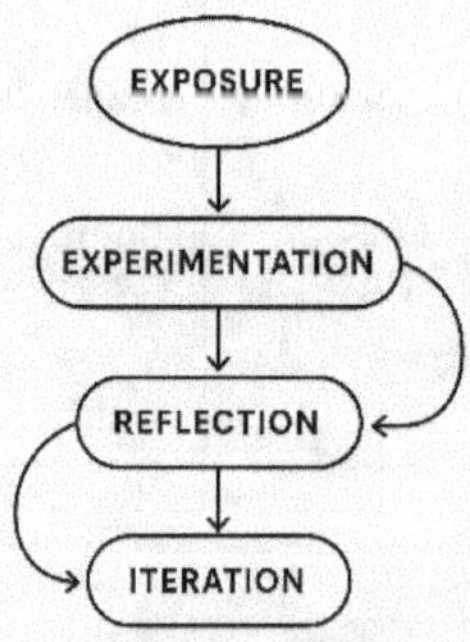

PROFESSIONAL
DEVELOPMENT
FEEDBACK LOOP

School-Wide PD Blueprint for AI Integration

A strong professional development (PD) plan supports not just tool use, but a deeper understanding of AI's role in learning.

Phase 1: Awareness and Framing (Month 1–3)

- Intro to AI in education: ethics, opportunities, and risks
- Classroom demos from early adopters
- Reflection sessions: "What could this solve in your practice?"

Phase 2: Skills and Use Cases (Month 4–6)

- Subject-specific AI integration workshops
- Role-specific sessions for counselors, principals, aides
- Collaborative lesson planning with AI tools

Phase 3: Coaching and Scaling (Month 7–12)

- In-class coaching and co-teaching support
- Peer-led workshops and problem-solving circles
- Documentation of wins, pitfalls, and emerging best practices

The 12-Month AI-Readiness Roadmap

This roadmap offers a sustainable timeline to move from exploration to confidence. It's not just about implementation—it's about alignment, reflection, and momentum.

Q1: Explore

- Form an AI leadership team
- Conduct staff and student readiness surveys
- Select 1–2 pilot tools aligned with strategic goals

Q2: Experiment

- Launch pilots in select classrooms or departments
- Host monthly reflection sessions
- Begin building a shared glossary and tool library

Q3: Evaluate

- Collect qualitative and quantitative feedback
- Adjust pilots based on student outcomes
- Host community night on AI in learning

Q4: Expand

- Broaden access to successful tools
- Launch school-wide PD refresh
- Set new goals for year 2 based on year 1 lessons

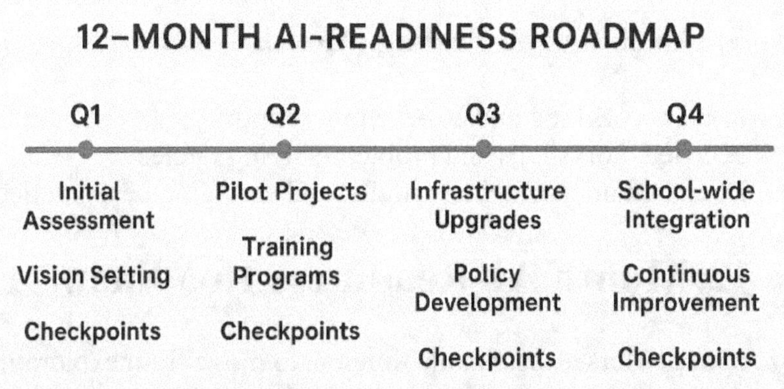

Tactical Best Practices for Building AI-Ready Culture

- **Start small, think long.** Don't aim for 100% adoption in year one—aim for 100% trust.
- **Give permission to pause.** Normalize uncertainty and experimentation.
- **Celebrate curiosity.** Highlight risk-takers, not just "tech experts."
- **Link tools to values.** Tie AI to your mission, not just metrics.
- **Measure what matters.** Focus on engagement, equity, and learning—not usage stats alone.

Common Pitfalls to Avoid

- **Confusing compliance with culture.** Attendance in PD ≠ belief or behavior change.
- **Isolating AI in the IT department.** This is a whole-school conversation, not a tech silo.
- **Overloading with tools.** One meaningful tool is better than five half-used ones.
- **Forgetting the "why."** Always connect AI integration to student success, not novelty.

Checklist: Is Your School Culture AI-Ready?

- Staff understand what AI is (and isn't) in education
- Teachers feel invited—not forced—to explore new tools
- PD supports reflection, not just skills training
- Student voice is part of pilot evaluation
- Leadership uses AI visibly and meaningfully
- Roadmap is documented and shared with all stakeholders

Conclusion

The most important technology in any school is still its people. Building an AI-ready culture doesn't mean everyone becomes a data scientist. It means building trust, curiosity, and clarity into every step of the journey. When teachers feel supported, students benefit. When leadership aligns vision with practice, innovation sticks. The future of AI in education isn't about tools—it's about transformation, together.

Next Steps

Technology should elevate *every* learner. In **Chapter 13: Equity and AI in Public Education**, we turn to the big question: Who's being left behind? We'll unpack digital divides, funding models, and practical ways to ensure rural and low-income schools don't miss the AI moment.

Chapter 13: Equity and AI in Public Education

AI is poised to transform education—but only for those who can access it. While many schools are piloting adaptive platforms, smart classrooms, and real-time analytics, others are still struggling with basic internet access or functioning devices. The risk isn't that AI will fail; it's that it will succeed *unevenly*, widening gaps between the already-resourced and those historically left behind.

This chapter tackles the equity imperative at the heart of educational AI. We explore the digital divide, rural and low-income school access, funding models that actually work, and how educators and communities can advocate for change. If AI is to serve *all* students, equity can't be a side concern—it must be built into every policy, product, and partnership from the start.

The Digital Divide in the Age of AI

The term "digital divide" no longer refers only to access to devices. It now encompasses:

- **Connectivity quality**: Broadband vs. limited or unreliable access
- **Device availability**: One-to-one device programs vs. shared or outdated equipment
- **Tech readiness**: Digital fluency among students, families, and teachers
- **AI literacy**: Knowing how to evaluate and use AI responsibly

When AI enters the classroom, these divides are compounded. Without equitable infrastructure, the very tools designed to personalize learning can instead amplify inequality.

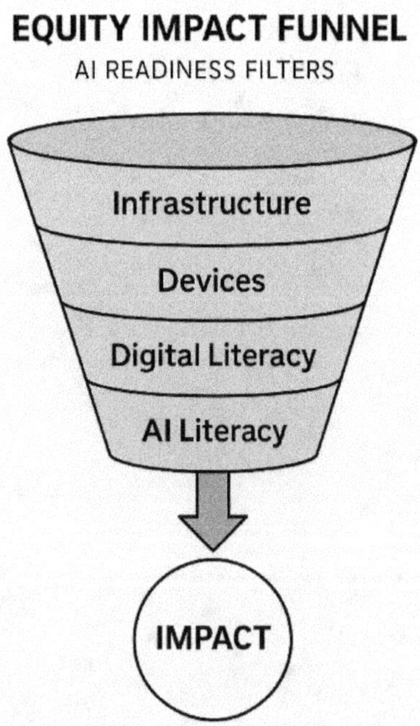

Risks for Rural and Low-Income Schools

AI requires more than just software licenses. Implementation depends on bandwidth, training, policy support, and ongoing technical assistance—all areas where underfunded districts struggle.

Common Barriers

- **Lack of consistent IT support**
- **Outdated procurement processes**
- **Insufficient training budgets for teachers**
- **Low community trust in data use or surveillance technologies**

Even when free or subsidized tools are available, these schools often lack the capacity to implement them effectively.

Hidden Cost of Inequity

When some students use AI to improve reading skills, practice advanced math, or receive early mental health alerts—while others don't—that's not a tech gap. It's an opportunity gap with lifelong consequences.

What Works: Funding Models and Strategic Partnerships

Equity in AI access doesn't mean giving every school the same tools—it means giving every student the right *opportunities* to benefit. Here's what's working on the ground:

1. Public–Private Partnerships

Tech companies are increasingly forming partnerships with school districts to provide:

- Subsidized access to adaptive platforms
- Professional development for teachers
- Infrastructure upgrades (e.g., Wi-Fi expansion)

But these must be structured with **community input and transparency** to avoid vendor lock-in or misaligned goals.

2. State-Level AI Innovation Grants

Some state education departments have launched competitive funding for AI pilot programs—particularly for Title I schools. These include:

- Implementation stipends
- Dedicated training budgets
- Evaluation frameworks that center equity

3. Local Foundations and Nonprofits

Regional organizations are stepping in to bridge gaps where state or federal support falls short. They often fund:

- Family-facing tech literacy programs
- Culturally responsive AI curriculum development
- Devices and hotspots for underserved students

Sample Programs and Funding Initiatives Across Rural, Urban, and Low-Income Districts

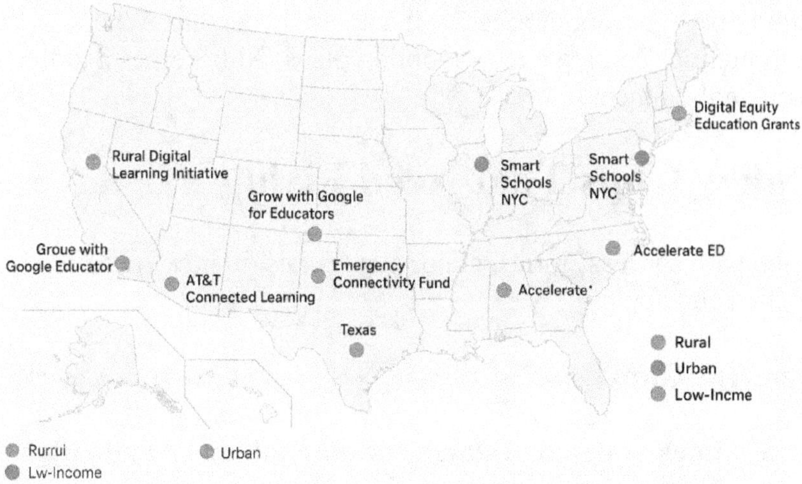

Real-World Example: Rural AI Integration in Kentucky

What Happened

A regional education cooperative in eastern Kentucky launched a pilot to bring adaptive learning tools to 12 rural districts. Using a blend of state grant funding and a private broadband partner, they rolled out AI literacy tools and teacher training over 18 months.

What Went Right

- Teacher-led PD ensured local relevance and trust
- Offline-compatible tools were prioritized
- Community tech nights built parent engagement

Within a year, schools reported higher student engagement in math and ELA—and 73% of teachers said they felt more confident using AI tools.

What We Learn from It

Equity isn't just about access—it's about ownership. When communities co-create tech adoption plans, AI becomes a tool *with* them, not *on* them.

Policy Gaps That Need Fixing

Even with success stories, major gaps persist in how AI policy is written and applied.

Current Gaps

- **Lack of national standards for equitable AI adoption**
- **No mandate for cultural bias testing in edtech algorithms**
- **Inconsistent state-level guidance on AI and student privacy**
- **Procurement barriers that favor large, expensive vendors**

What Advocates Can Do

- **Push for equity impact reports** before adopting new AI tools
- **Support legislation** that funds AI access in underserved districts
- **Build coalitions** with parents, teachers, and local leaders
- **Engage school boards** with data and community stories

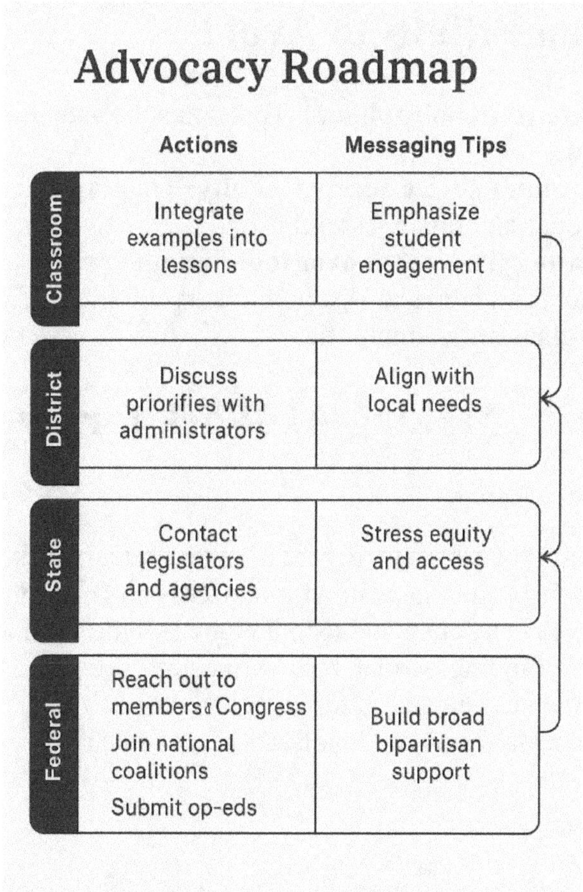

Tactical Best Practices for Equity-Driven AI Integration

- **Start with infrastructure audits**: Know what each school needs before buying software
- **Involve families and students**: Co-design tech plans and communication strategies
- **Prioritize tools with low-bandwidth modes**: Accessibility matters more than flash
- **Demand clear bias-testing documentation** from vendors
- **Support educator peer-learning networks** in under-resourced areas

Common Pitfalls to Avoid

- **One-size-fits-all rollouts**: Tools must be adapted for local needs
- **Assuming device access = equity**: Training, relevance, and support are equally essential
- **Chasing flashy tech over foundational access**
- **Ignoring historical distrust** of surveillance or data misuse in marginalized communities

Checklist: Making AI Work for Every Learner

- Audit your district's digital infrastructure, by school
- Identify equity gaps in AI tool access and outcomes
- Prioritize training and tech literacy in Title I schools
- Build funding partnerships with equity safeguards
- Center student and family voice in AI decisions
- Advocate for policy that treats access as a right—not a luxury

Conclusion

AI in education must be more than innovation for the well-funded. If we don't prioritize equity now, the digital divide will become an AI divide—one that reinforces the very inequities schools are meant to overcome. But with the right partnerships, funding models, and advocacy, we can ensure every student—not just the lucky few—gets a seat at the future of learning.

Next Steps

Equity starts with leadership. In **Chapter 14: Leading the Shift — Traits of AI-Forward Educators**, we'll explore what makes a teacher or school leader ready to guide others into the age of AI. From adaptability and curiosity to scalable microtraining, we'll look at how to build a team of champions from the inside out.

Chapter 14: Leading the Shift — Traits of AI-Forward Educators

AI integration in schools doesn't begin with a platform or a policy. It begins with people—specifically, educators who lead with curiosity, adaptability, and a clear sense of purpose. These "AI-forward" educators are not always the most tech-savvy or the loudest voices in the room. More often, they are the ones asking, "How could this improve student learning?" and "How can we try this responsibly?"

As AI reshapes everything from instruction to operations, schools need leaders at every level—teachers, coaches, principals—who can guide their teams through change without fear or burnout. This chapter defines the core traits of AI-forward educators, offers a model for identifying and growing AI champions, and showcases a simple, scalable strategy already making waves: the "AI Lunch & Learn" movement.

Who Are AI-Forward Educators?

AI-forward educators aren't defined by job title—they're defined by mindset. These are the individuals who move past tool adoption into culture-building. They translate new technologies into practical strategies. And most importantly, they inspire *others* to take the leap.

Core Traits

- **Vision**: They see beyond today's classroom needs and align AI use with long-term student success.
- **Curiosity**: They ask questions, explore tools, and model lifelong learning.
- **Adaptability**: They pivot gracefully as tools evolve, policies shift, or pilots reveal surprises.
- **Digital Comfort**: They aren't necessarily experts—but they're comfortable experimenting, failing forward, and learning in public.

These educators are often the connective tissue between leadership vision and teacher practice.

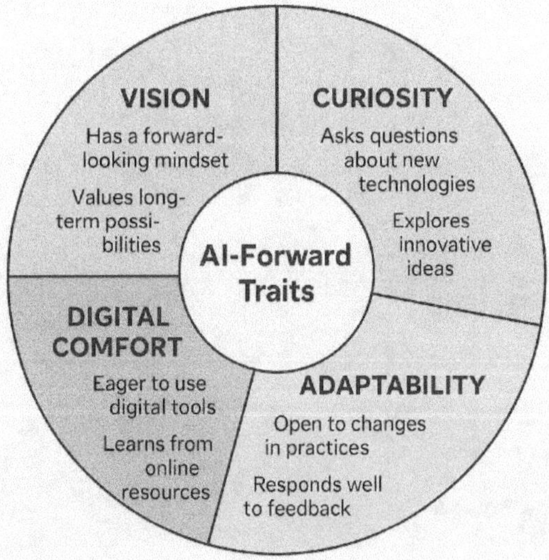

Creating AI Champions in Your School

One of the most effective change strategies is identifying and supporting "champions"—educators who can lead by example, support peers, and translate vision into classroom action.

How to Identify a Champion

- Volunteers for tech pilots—not just because they love tools, but because they care about solving problems
- Asks students how tools impact their experience
- Offers informal help to colleagues or mentors new staff
- Reflects openly on successes *and* failures

How to Support Them

- Offer professional development that goes *beyond* tool usage—focus on pedagogy, ethics, and design thinking
- Give them time: release periods, stipends, or lighter duties during key pilot phases
- Empower them to lead PD sessions or host open-classroom days
- Recognize their leadership *publicly*, not just privately

Microtraining That Scales

Traditional PD often fails because it's too long, too general, or too disconnected from daily teaching. Microtraining flips the model: short, focused sessions led by peers, with immediate relevance.

Microtraining Best Practices

- **Length**: 20–30 minutes, max
- **Format**: Hands-on, interactive, scenario-based
- **Delivery**: In department meetings, PLCs, or before/after school
- **Follow-Up**: Offer a "use it this week" challenge or classroom coaching

Examples:

- "Using ChatGPT to Generate Reading Prompts for Diverse Learners"
- "AI-Powered Formative Feedback in Google Classroom"
- "How to Spot Bias in AI-Recommended Lesson Plans"

Microtraining Session

TOPIC	AI Tips for Social Studies
AUDIENCE	Middle school social studies teachers
GOALS	– Share ideas for instructional use – Encourage experimentation
FOLLOW-UP ACTIONS	– Start an online discussion thread – Collect feedback from teachers

Case Study: The "AI Lunch & Learn" Movement

What Happened

At a mid-sized K–12 district in Minnesota, a group of teachers started hosting informal "AI Lunch & Learn" sessions in the library once a week. Each session focused on one tool, one challenge, and one real classroom example. Teachers brought their lunch, their laptops, and their questions.

What Went Right

- Attendance grew organically through word of mouth
- Newer teachers felt empowered to share and lead
- Trust built faster than in formal PD settings
- Several attendees became district-level AI leads within a year

The format was low-pressure but high-impact—making AI adoption feel approachable, not mandated.

What We Learn from It

Sometimes, the best training doesn't come from a consultant—it comes from a colleague down the hall. When educators feel safe to explore and supported to lead, adoption spreads naturally.

Tactical Best Practices for Cultivating AI-Forward Leadership

- **Ask who's already leading quietly.** Champions may not have titles—but they have trust.
- **Embed training in existing structures.** PLCs, grade-level meetings, common planning time.
- **Encourage co-teaching and peer demos.** Seeing AI in use beats hearing about it.
- **Celebrate small wins.** Early adopters need recognition to stay motivated.
- **Build a feedback loop.** Ask champions what support they need—and give it.

Common Pitfalls to Avoid

- **Assigning leadership without buy-in.** Champions must volunteer, not be voluntold.
- **Assuming digital fluency = leadership.** Tech-savvy doesn't always mean pedagogically strong.
- **Waiting for "perfect" tools.** Leadership grows during exploration—not after rollout.
- **Overloading champions.** Give them time and resources to lead sustainably.

Checklist: Building a Network of AI-Forward Educators

- Identify 3–5 potential AI champions in your school
- Provide PD that focuses on mindset and strategy, not just tools
- Launch a microtraining program with clear goals
- Host informal AI events (e.g., Lunch & Learn, tool swaps, demo weeks)
- Create pathways for champions to influence school or district policy
- Publicly recognize leadership to reinforce culture

Conclusion

The future of education won't be led by algorithms. It will be led by educators with vision, adaptability, and the courage to try something new. AI-forward teachers don't need to know every tool—they need to know their *why*, stay curious, and bring others along. The shift is already underway. The question is: who will lead it?

Next Steps

The next chapter is the final one—but it looks forward. In **Chapter 15: The Future of Education — And How to Lead It**, we step into what's coming next: immersive classrooms, global learning paths, predictive planning. More than a forecast, it's a call to action. Let's end with a strategic vision for the schools we're building now—and the ones we haven't yet imagined.

Chapter 15: The Future of Education — And How to Lead It

The future of education is not ahead of us—it's unfolding right now. In classrooms where students collaborate with AI tutors, in schools where predictive data guides career readiness, and in districts reimagining credentials for a global stage, the transformation is already happening. The tools are no longer hypothetical. The shift is no longer optional.

This final chapter brings everything together: emerging technologies, structural shifts, and leadership strategies that will define the next decade of learning. It's a call to action—not for tech adoption alone, but for purpose-driven innovation that expands opportunity, equity, and human potential.

The Tech Stack of Tomorrow's Classrooms

When we talk about "future-ready" learning environments, we're not just talking about AI. We're talking about a convergence of exponential technologies—each adding a new layer to how, where, and why students learn.

AI + AR/VR + IoT + Blockchain

- **AI**: Personalizes instruction, automates assessment, enables predictive analytics
- **AR/VR**: Immerses students in virtual labs, historical simulations, or multilingual conversations
- **IoT (Internet of Things)**: Connects physical learning spaces through sensors, wearables, and smart devices that adjust lighting, sound, or content based on student behavior
- **Blockchain**: Secures learning credentials, stores microlearning records, and enables portable, verifiable transcripts

Together, these technologies move education from passive content delivery to dynamic, data-informed, immersive learning ecosystems.

Predictive Pathways: Career Mapping and Microcredentials

Future education isn't just about engagement—it's about *preparation.* Students are entering a workforce in flux, where job titles change faster than curriculum cycles. That's where predictive and modular learning paths come in.

Predictive Career Mapping

Using student performance data, interest inventories, and local labor market trends, AI can:

- Suggest career paths aligned with strengths and goals
- Recommend relevant coursework, extracurriculars, and certifications
- Surface internship or apprenticeship opportunities before graduation

Microcredentials and Global Access

Instead of waiting four years for a diploma, students earn **microcredentials**—verifiable badges for mastering discrete skills like:

- Data literacy
- Digital citizenship
- Creative problem-solving
- Industry-specific tools (e.g., CAD, video editing, coding languages)

These credentials can be stacked, shared globally, and used in both academic and professional portfolios.

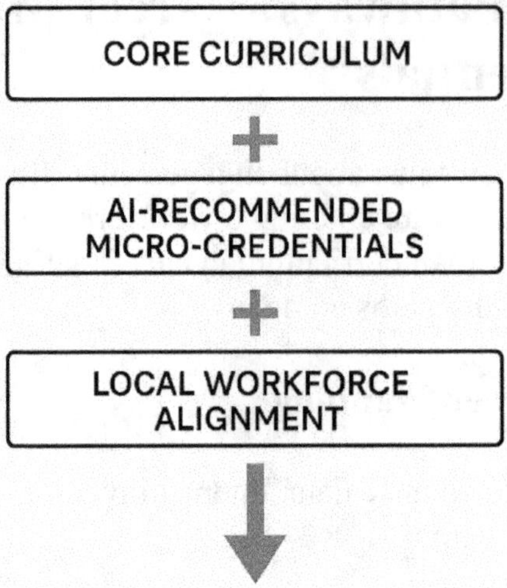

The 5-Year Strategic Plan for School Leaders

Change doesn't happen all at once. But it *can* be led with purpose. Here's a practical 5-year roadmap for leaders looking to future-proof their schools.

Year 1: Vision + Audit

- Build a cross-functional innovation team
- Assess current infrastructure, staffing, and curriculum gaps
- Define your "why" for adopting emerging tech

Year 2: Pilot + Feedback

- Launch 2–3 tech pilots tied to core challenges (e.g., reading, retention, access)
- Collect teacher, student, and family feedback
- Begin AI and digital literacy training for all staff

Year 3: Scale + Align

- Expand successful pilots school-wide
- Align new tech with SEL, DEI, and career readiness goals
- Develop early versions of microcredential programs

Year 4: Integrate + Report

- Integrate AI and IoT tools into curriculum planning cycles
- Launch student data dashboards with privacy controls
- Host community events to share outcomes and stories

Year 5: Sustain + Lead

- Establish a district-wide innovation office or future learning council
- Share your model with peer schools or at state-level forums
- Mentor other districts and contribute to policy discussions

5-Year Strategic Leadership Timeline

Year	Goal	Milestones	Outcome measures
Year 1	**Assess Current State**	Conduct needs analysis Benchmark AI readiness	Alaseliness completed
Year 2	**Set Vision and Strategy**	Define AI goals Allocate initial resources Form leadership team	AI strategic plan developed
Year 3	**Pilot AI Initiatives**	Launch pilot projects Train educators Gather feedback	Pilot results evaluated
Year 4	**Scale Successful Programs**	Expand AI implementation Increase investment Document best practices	AI programs scaled up
Year 5	**Sustain and Innovate**	Review progress Update AI strategy Explore new technologies	Long-term impact demonstrated

Final Message: The Transformation Is Already Here

This is not about chasing trends—it's about answering to the needs of a generation that expects more. More personalization. More relevance. More connection to the world they'll inherit.

AI will not replace educators. But it will reshape what it means to be one. Classrooms will still need empathy, curiosity, humor, and care. What's changing is the *scale* at which we can deliver those things—and the *tools* we use to ensure no student is left behind.

You don't need to become an expert in every emerging technology. You need to lead with clarity, ask better questions, and empower others to explore with confidence.

The future of education isn't five years away. It's already underway. You are not preparing for it—you are shaping it.

Thank you for being part of the shift.

THE END

CHECK YOUR BONUS AT THE END !

Glossary: AI and the Future of Education

AI (Artificial Intelligence)

A field of computer science that enables machines to perform tasks that typically require human intelligence, such as learning, reasoning, and problem-solving. In education, AI powers tools for grading, personalized learning, and predictive analytics.

Adaptive Learning

A method of instruction powered by AI that adjusts content, pacing, and difficulty in real time based on a student's performance, preferences, and engagement level.

AI-Forward Educator

A school leader or teacher who embodies curiosity, adaptability, and digital fluency. These educators champion responsible AI use, lead peer learning, and connect emerging tools to instructional goals.

AI Literacy

The ability to understand, critique, and interact responsibly with AI systems. Includes knowledge of how AI works, its limits, ethical concerns, and its role in shaping society and learning.

AI-Ready School Culture

A school environment where staff and leadership embrace innovation through training, experimentation, and aligned values. It includes clear purpose, peer-driven PD, and a roadmap for integration.

AR/VR (Augmented Reality/Virtual Reality)

Immersive technologies used in classrooms to create interactive experiences. AR overlays digital content on the real world; VR creates fully simulated environments for learning.

Blockchain in Education

A decentralized, secure way to store and verify academic credentials, microcredentials, and student records. Ensures tamper-proof, portable documentation of learning.

ChatGPT

An AI language model developed by OpenAI that can generate, summarize, translate, and assist in writing tasks. In schools, it's used for tutoring, content generation, and student engagement—but must be guided by ethical use policies.

Digital Divide

The gap between individuals who have access to modern information and communication technology (like broadband and devices) and those who do not. A key equity issue in AI deployment.

Emotion AI

Also known as affective computing, this technology interprets facial expressions, voice tones, and other cues to assess emotional states. Used in some schools for early intervention—but controversial due to privacy concerns.

Equity in AI

The principle that all students, regardless of background, should benefit from AI-enhanced learning. Requires conscious attention to access, representation, bias mitigation, and community trust.

Explainability (in AI)

The ability of an AI system to make its decision-making process understandable to humans. Critical in education for transparency and accountability in grading, feedback, or predictions.

Formative Feedback

Ongoing, timely feedback provided to students during the learning process—often AI-assisted—to guide improvement before final assessment.

Gamification

The application of game design principles (points, levels, rewards) to non-game contexts. Tools like Classcraft use gamification to increase student engagement.

Human-in-the-Loop (HITL)

An AI design principle where humans oversee, validate, or override AI decisions. In schools, HITL ensures teachers remain the final decision-makers on grading, interventions, and learning paths.

IoT (Internet of Things)

A network of connected devices that collect and share data. In classrooms, IoT can include smartboards, environmental sensors, and wearables used to optimize learning environments.

Learning Analytics

The collection, measurement, and analysis of student data to improve instruction. Powered by AI, analytics can identify trends, predict dropout risk, or personalize learning.

Lunch & Learn

An informal professional development model where educators gather over lunch to explore a specific tool, topic, or strategy—often peer-led and focused on practical AI applications.

Microcredentials

Stackable, digital certifications for discrete skills or competencies. Unlike traditional degrees, microcredentials can be earned quickly and verified via blockchain for college or career use.

Microtraining

Short, focused PD sessions (typically 15–30 minutes) that target a specific skill or tool. Often delivered peer-to-peer and designed to scale organically across schools.

Personalized Learning

An instructional model that tailors learning experiences to the individual needs, interests, and pace of each student—often supported by AI tools.

Pilot Program

A time-bound, small-scale test of a new technology or strategy, used to gather feedback and assess feasibility before full-scale implementation.

Plagiarism Detection

AI tools that check student work for originality. Advanced systems can detect paraphrasing, idea similarity, or AI-generated writing.

Predictive Analytics

AI techniques that analyze patterns in student behavior and performance to forecast future outcomes (e.g., risk of dropout, college readiness).

Professional Development (PD) Blueprint

A structured plan for training staff in AI tools and mindsets, including phases like awareness, skill-building, coaching, and reflection.

Real-Time Feedback Loop

Systems that allow teachers or platforms to immediately respond to student input—adjusting content, offering support, or flagging disengagement.

Socratic Prompting

Using ChatGPT or other AI tools to simulate dialogue with historical or fictional figures, challenging students to think critically and explore multiple perspectives.

Smart Classroom

A technology-enhanced learning environment equipped with AI-powered tools, sensors, and interactive devices that adapt to student needs in real time.

Student Autonomy

The principle that students should have control over their learning data, decisions, and paths. Core to ethical AI design in schools.

Surveillance Creep

The gradual normalization of excessive monitoring in the name of safety or performance. A concern with emotion AI, facial recognition, or always-on tracking tools.

Transparency in AI

Ensuring that students, parents, and teachers understand how AI systems work, what data they collect, and how decisions are made.

Use Disclosure

A practice where students note when AI tools were used in their work—building ethical awareness and academic honesty.

Vision-Driven Adoption

Implementing AI not because it's available, but because it aligns with a clearly articulated mission to improve equity, engagement, and achievement.

Wellness Monitoring

AI-based systems that track student stress, engagement, and well-being. Promising but controversial, these tools must prioritize privacy, consent, and counselor oversight.

Bonus – FREE eBook Version

Want the full-color PDF version of this book?
Simply email me at **ericl@acrasolution.com** with a **screenshot of your Amazon purchase**, and I'll gladly send you your personal copy.

Thank you for taking the time to read this eBook.

Your support means more than you know. **By purchasing this book, you're directly contributing to the creation of more high-quality, practical resources** for business owners, IT leaders, and everyday professionals navigating the complex world of cybersecurity. It's because of readers like you that I can continue researching, writing, and delivering tools that make a real difference.

Whether you leave a positive review, recommend this book to a colleague, or simply apply what you've learned — **you're helping grow a stronger, safer business community. And for that, I sincerely thank you.**

At **AcraSolution**, we're committed to providing both premium services and a wide range of **free, actionable tools**. Our growing library includes documentation, articles, and step-by-step guides — designed to bring you immediate value, no strings attached.

If you need additional guidance or support, don't hesitate to visit our website www.acrasolution.com or reach out directly.

Together, we can build a more secure future.

— *Eric LeBouthillier*
Author & Cybersecurity Strategist

www.ingramcontent.com/pod-product-compliance
Lightning Source LLC
LaVergne TN
LVHW022059200926
848481LV00003B/989

* 9 7 8 1 0 6 9 6 4 3 7 3 5 *